P9-DOG-827

The CENTER *of the* UNIVERSE

The CENTER *of the* UNIVERSE

A Memoir

Nancy Bachrach

ALFRED A. KNOPF NEW YORK 2009

THIS IS A BORZOI BOOK
PUBLISHED BY ALFRED A. KNOPF

Published in the United States by Alfred A. Knopf,
a division of Random House, Inc., New York,
and in Canada by Random House of Canada Limited, Toronto.
www.aaknopf.com

Knopf, Borzoi Books, and the colophon are registered
trademarks of Random House, Inc.

Library of Congress Cataloging-in-Publication Data
Bachrach, Nancy.
The center of the universe : a memoir / Nancy Bachrach.
p. cm.
"A Borzoi book"—T.p. verso.
ISBN 978-0-307-27090-0
1. Bachrach, Nancy. 2. Bachrach, Nancy—Family. 3. Mothers and daughters—United States. 4. Mentally ill parents—United States—Biography. 5. Providence (R.I.)—Biography. 6. New York (N.Y.)—Biography. 7. Marketing—France—Paris—Biography. I. Title.
CT275.B134A3 2009
974.7'1043092—dc22
[B] 2008048770

Manufactured in the United States of America
First Edition

For Saint Orin
and the Toes Club

I sit astride life like a bad rider on a horse, and I owe it only to the horse's good nature that I am not thrown off at this very moment.

—LUDWIG WITTGENSTEIN

WOTAN:
Deathless woman!
Waken, waken!

ERDA:
Dazed am I
since I awoke
wild and strange
seems the World.

—RICHARD WAGNER

Contents

Author's Note

Memory is so fragile that even perspective can distort it, but this is a work of nonfiction, mostly about my mother. If she had written it, she'd have spun the material into a juicy novel, maybe an epic, because she loved invention and the lift of a good lie. But she also approved of my telling the truth, or as close to the truth as I've ever been able to get.

Resemblance to actual persons, living or dead, is largely unavoidable in a true story, due to the nature of reality. So names have been changed, and events have been gently reshuffled—something they do on their own anyway, over time. A few living persons have been airbrushed, but the dead were fair game—and although my pen is a blunt instrument, no one was actually killed in the making of this book.

The CENTER *of the* UNIVERSE

ONE

Things Fall Apart

MEMORIAL DAY WEEKEND, 1983

In the ancient forest on the Right Bank of Paris lies a jewel-like island where Napoleon, just back from the Alps, built a Swiss chalet. Emerald lawns and ruby flowers shimmer beside a sapphire lake as peacocks stride by. On a sunny Sunday morning in May, I am ensconced on the chalet's terrace, now a café, replenishing more energy than my leisurely jog has exhausted. Around me, lazy hands stir sugar cubes in slow circles and spread butter on crusty baguettes. These are the only signs of industry in a city where the principal exercises are digestion and strolling, where laissez-faire is practiced and preached, where intermission is the pace of life.

I saunter through the woods toward my apartment as the ladies of the night flee daylight like vampires stumbling upon a cross. I know one of the Brazilians by name, since I pass her most mornings as she's wrapping up her night's work in tissues. Alexandro has just become Alexandra. Like her, I came to Paris to reinvent myself three years ago. Although I had no surgery, I did change my name, and while no one calls me a prostitute, sometimes I feel like one, admittedly, in another old and unlofty profession, advertising.

I've been relocated from headquarters in New York to tackle a marketing emergency for an important toiletries client—the launch of France's first, sorely needed antiperspirant. Our team on the Seine—ninety-nine people smoking and loitering above a gas station—won the coveted assignment (code-named Stink-o) even though they've failed for a decade to browbeat their countrymen into American bar soap. Which is why someone very high up at bar soap headquarters, someone with a good nose but a rarely used passport, smells an untapped market for deodorants over here, and although I can imagine the logic that led to this conclusion (and my relocation), the person who reached it hasn't had to sit through forty focus groups in unventilated conference rooms in the provinces. Getting the natives to "adopt" a roll-on, stick, or spray will require "a paradigm shift," I'm learning, a long and winding road that's synonymous with a huge media budget and then, usually, failure. What would make the French—who relish the bleu on their cheese and their skin, who have a whole class of things they fondly call "stinky"—what would make them plug up their pores with wax to placate and enrich our big American client? This is the onerous marketing dilemma I face daily in my otherwise idyllic life in the City of Light.

To help me think through the Stink-o conundrum, I have the Semis—a squadron of French semiologists, not just translators but also linguists and cogitators, who are deconstructing the semantics of our antiperspirancy muddle. Not solving it exactly, just scrutinizing it in the Gallic way, ad nauseam. For my edification, the Semis are writing a treatise on perspiration, its cultural heritage, its evolutionary value, its distillation of primeval body essences. My task is to develop a successful campaign against sweat, when it rivals the madeleine in the collective olfactory unconscious.

Tucked behind a manicured garden in the Sixteenth Arrondissement is the elegant *rue* where I live—in a Beaux-Arts town house with a tiny filigreed elevator, where I would imagine Maurice Chevalier crooning to Leslie Caron even if "Gigi" weren't playing on the concierge's stereo. From my apartment on the top floor—four rooms with high ceilings and crown moldings, eight times the size of my New York studio, thanks to the value of the dollar under Reagan—there's a postcard view of the tip of the Eiffel Tower, which I am admiring through open windows, when my phone rings.

The connection has a bad echo, so it's an overseas call, although it's two in the morning in the States.

Surely, as the poet said, *some revelation is at hand*.

My brother, Ben, weeping hello, sounds both frantic and measured. He tells me he has "terrible news." He says I'd better "prepare" myself.

I have never had any idea what to do after someone says "prepare yourself," since the warning itself is an angst infusion.

"*Sssxxzzz* is dead," Ben says, but the ocean is sloshing against underwater cables, making puddles of noise in his words.

"*Who? Who's* dead?" This is the moment when time collapses, when what hasn't yet been said feels like déjà vu.

"*DAD!*" he shouts. "*DAD* is dead."

The echo repeats his words. "Dad is dead—*dad is dead*."

Our father is fifty-eight—a vigorous, athletic, handsome fifty-eight. "Boyish" is the first thing people call him, not always as a compliment.

"Dad is *dead?* How?"

"The boat—*the boat*."

That is explanation enough.

Facing me is a photo of our father aboard his secondhand fourteen-year-old "cabin cruiser," the *Mr. Fix It*, unwrapping my last birthday gift—an inflatable life raft. Spouting the Coast Guard motto, *Semper Paratus*, he is, or was, constantly fiddling with nautical instruments whose failures are legendary. Last year's close call came fifty miles off Martha's Vineyard, with no land in sight, when he and my mother happened upon a "sudden" storm—which functioning radar or a transistor radio would have disclosed. It swept the deck furniture overboard and almost did the same to them before they strapped themselves into their seats. So it is easy to picture Mr. Fix It himself chomping on a cigar like Ralph Kramden, piloting blind from his flying bridge under a starless sky, next to a mute radio, as an unforeseen tidal wave washes over his boat (again) and drags him into the Atlantic. I glimpse his black hair bobbing in the ocean and his hands flailing as a shark circles and pokes him in the chest.

> *The blood-dimmed tide is loosed, and everywhere*
> *The ceremony of innocence is drowned . . .*

"He *drowned?*"

"No, it was carbon monoxide. Dad was asphyxiated."

I see my father get down on his knees in the galley, where he opens the oven door and puts his head inside. Resting his cheek on the oven rack, just for a moment. Deciding. He reaches for the knobs and turns them on, one at a time, and, squeezing his eyes shut, he takes a deep breath.

But the only oven on his boat is a toaster.

"How did he do it?"

"It was an accident. And Mom was with him. She's in a coma."

The second shoe. *The widening gyre.*

"How long will Mom be in the coma?" I ask stupidly. I have

always trusted in the omniscience of doctors, especially when the doctor is my brother. Ben is a lung specialist in New York's busiest emergency room, with a need to come to the rescue so old and so deep that only triage at Bellevue seems to satisfy it.

"I've done everything I can. It's out of my hands."

I am afraid to ask whose hands it's in now. "Can I make it home in time?"

"She's in a little Catholic hospital at the beach for Chrissake."

Meaning what? Is this code for pulling the plug? Or for not being able to pull the plug? I want to ask, but I don't want to ask—having come of age in the sixties, I always assume my phone is tapped. So I keep that thought and a whole stomachache of fears to myself—while I try not to think about Sunny von Bülow.

"I hate to say this—I know it's awful—but you've got to *prepare yourself* for a double funeral."

How do I prepare for a double funeral? Pack two of everything? Pack clothes that are *very* black? The unimaginable has just happened, and the unpredictable is around the corner, and it feels like I missed my chance to prepare.

My brain screens an improvised documentary short, like a practice drill. His and hers coffins roll off an assembly line. Their sides touch in a final wooden embrace; then they linger at the edge of a double grave—a deep pocket of dirt for two. The Mourner's Kaddish is sung, and God is glorified and sanctified for no reason I've ever been able to discern during a funeral. And then the twin boxes tip into the breach, headfirst or feetfirst—impossible to know which; maybe one of each.

Long drum roll. Fade to very black.

Telling the story in an orderly way oversimplifies it, since truth is less tidy than prose, and maybe less plausible. Were Madame

Defarge to knit the narrative, the yarn would have a dark side and a light side, and it would flip itself over and over—a tale of quick reversals—full of snags and dropped stitches and tangled threads. Frayed and raggedy, perhaps, but lively nonetheless.

I began taking notes for a story about my mother the minute I could write. I wrote everywhere—on my school desk and in the margins of my books and notebooks, on paper napkins and garbage bags when there were no pads around because she was using all of them, and eventually into one diary after another. There are things I didn't write down—not every story needs to be told—but I recorded plenty.

On my dresser is a family photo from the fifties, of me with Ben and our little sister, Helen. We're sitting closer than we need to be in the spacious backseat of our father's yellow Chevy, dressed identically in crisp white shirts and khaki shorts, three small slightly green faces—six, eight, and ten—set against the smoky haze of an airtight sedan. We're on the road to summer camp in the Catskills, in uniform, with our father, Mort, behind the wheel, blowing smoke rings. Frank Sinatra is singing "Stardust" on the radio.

And now the purple dusk of twilight time
Steals across the meadows of my heart
High up in the sky the little stars climb
Always reminding me that we're apart.

Our mother, Lola, has been asleep, with her head in Mort's lap, but she wakes up spring-loaded: Her auburn curls pop up above the seat, followed by an incandescent smile. Glancing down at us in the back, she blows a theatrical kiss and gets ready to tell us a story.

"I was dreaming," the story begins.

She waits until everyone is paying attention. Mort turns off the radio.

"I am the center of the universe," she says, looking at each of us in turn, making sure we appreciate the significance. "And everyone else is a star revolving around me."

This is a confession. A revelation. A pronouncement. This is the way of the world.

She is Norma Desmond, descending the staircase in *Sunset Boulevard*, eyes wide and frozen, getting ready for her close-up. She is Salome, stripping the veil off the face of the cosmos. She is my mother, Lola Hornstein.

And she is crazy.

Twirling her fingers in dainty arcs, she demonstrates the rotation of the solar system around her, right there in the front seat. Cupping her hands lovingly around a star to bring it closer, basking in its reflected light. She is Pivotal, the axis of a magical orbit, spinning, spinning, while the rest of us are drawn to her by gravity.

I am as weightless as dust, sucked into her vacuum.

She giggles, then blushes, and her hands leave their stellar rotation to stifle a laugh. Then she chuckles and cackles until she roars.

"Cut it out, Lola." Mort is weary.

"I am the brightest star," she insists, peeved, since it's obvious that my father doesn't get it yet, that he needs further clarification.

But *I* get it: Lola could burn out fast, or she could burn out slowly. The speed is unknowable, but it's certain that a firestorm is coming. And then it will get very dark.

"But it was only a dream," Mort says.

"It was a *vision*!" she responds grandly, infuriated by his impertinence. "I AM THE CENTER OF THE UNIVERSE!"

Widening her sphere of influence to enclose all of us, she

swirls her arms majestically, and her hand grazes the wheel accidentally, making the car veer into the next lane.

Mort pushes her away.

"Knock it off. I'm driving." He sounds angry now. I'll bet he's scared, too.

"I *command* you to stop this car!"

He glances over at her, then back at the road, noncommittal, and turns the radio back on.

Love is now the stardust of yesterday
The music of the years gone by.

"I'm talking to you, mister. You'd better stop this damn car right now, because I'm getting out."

I'm rooting for getting out, too, and soon. But Mort doesn't follow orders. Mort thinks he's in charge.

So Lola leans over and reminds him *who* is the center of the universe—she beats his chest like a tom-tom, chanting that she hates him. She's very convincing.

Down the two-lane road we drift, while Mort tries to bring Lola and the Chevy under control. Finally, he pulls over to the breakdown lane, and the right wheels end up on a grassy embankment like a Tilt-A-Whirl, so what seemed lopsided only a moment ago now truly *is*.

Lola throws her door open and runs off in her yellow sundress and sandals, weaving through thick hedges at the side of the road.

"Why is Mommy playing hide-and-seek?" my little sister asks.

Traffic slows down as people lean out their car windows, pointing at my father, who's running after my mother, who's puking tuna fish on rye, no extra mayo, please, in the bushes. When he catches her, he grabs her by the shoulders and wipes vomit off her chin with his sleeve. Then he leads her back to the car, puts her in her side, and locks her door.

Lola looks at herself in the visor mirror and reapplies her lipstick, moving the brassy tube around and around and around her thick red lips, getting ready for the next scene.

"Okay, everything's fine now," Mort announces as he gets in, transferring tuna vomit from his shirt to the front seat.

We are halfway to Camp High Peak, three hungry birds in a wobbly nest, imprinting on an ostrich with his head in the sand while a wild hyena nips at his tail.

For the next two hours, Lola delivers celestial updates, hysterically. Announcing the astronomical news, she nods to Gemini on her way to Virgo. And although she chides the moon for crossing in front of her, she permits Cassiopeia to carry her train. She fashions a necklace of aurora borealis before destroying it and ordering an eclipse.

I am a captive audience, absorbed by her, entranced by the star turn in the front seat. Meanwhile, the Chevy winds up the Taconic Parkway and around a mountain road, the recipe for nausea, and Mort has to stop a second time for a round of family retching.

When we get to camp, the three of us scatter the instant our car is unloaded. While the other kids are clinging to their parents, pleading with them not to go, I beg my father to take my mother and leave. To get rid of the evidence that I am not normal. I don't care whether he takes her to a hospital or a jail cell or just back to the living room, where he can continue to tell everyone there's nothing really wrong with her. "She's just under too much pressure, is all."

Mort is always telling people their problems are in their heads. Backache? In your head. Constipation? In your head. Migraines? Definitely in your head. But when it comes to Lola, there's nothing *really* wrong in her head. "She's just under too much pressure, is all." All Lola needs is a road trip.

In the photo she stuffed into my camp trunk, lest I forget her for even a moment, Lola and Mort strike a madcap pose. He, in tweed pants, is bent over, rear to camera, with his head in the shadow between her legs; she is grinning at the camera, is leaning her elbows on his ass, like she owns him from the waist down. Her head, his tail—one zany bowlegged sepia parent-creature.

Weeks pass without a word from either of them, although Lola usually writes nonstop, dashing off ditties on ragged slips of paper and tucking them into my books, drawers, lunches, pockets, and pillows. She reads at least a book a day and would probably write one, too, if there were ever enough blank paper around the house. The hutch in the dining room is a library of her unpublished manuscripts—poems, plays, parodies, musicals, and jingles. Plus the first few chapters of a novel—of several novels.

In the mess hall, I spot Ben and Helen from a distance. Ben's on the boys' side of the room, as though camp is an Orthodox shul, and Helen sits in a special roped-off section that's for kids who are too young to be at camp in the first place. She's been cast as Baby June in the camp production of *Gypsy*, and after she tap-dances her way through the first act, she's marched off to bed before the strippers take the stage in act 2. We rarely have a chance to speak, which is just as well. I wouldn't know what to say. The minute I see either of them, Lola's red curls spring up unbidden, and I want to run the other way.

In search of a surrogate mother, I develop a needy attachment to my counselor, Sylvia Feldman, a nineteen-year-old philosophy major at Smith. I curry favor and declare exorbitant love, but she has no idea what to make of me. She informs me, in fact, that she "can't be certain of my existence unless I prove my will is stronger than hers." This is heady stuff, but the daughter of the center of the universe is up to it.

So I put Sylvia to the test right away. That's how I learn that her credo is all double-talk, since the proof I offer of my strong will—honing my talent for insurrection by beating up two bigger girls and rolling up my sleeves for a third—gets me expelled to the softball field, where she marches me around the bases until dark. But at least we are together.

On the night before Visiting Day, long after lights out, I lie awake, afraid to go to sleep, wondering whether Mort will show up with Lola in the morning and whether she'll kill herself when she gets here. I'm afraid she will, and I'm afraid she won't. My heart's going bump in the night, while nine little girls sleep peacefully near my snoring, adored Sylvia.

I pull a blanket over my head, but someone yanks it off, shakes my shoulder, whispers my name. It's the middle of the night, and it's freezing, but Mort is here, and he's agitated. I'd better pack up right now, he tells me—he's driven three hundred miles, and everybody has to go home with him this minute. And he'd better get his money back, or all hell will break loose.

Didn't all hell break loose a while ago?

"Let's go," he says, "Right now."

I would sooner eat glass than go home with him. Lola is home.

But then I hear her voice, booming from the rafters, like the voice of God. "You are coming with us, and you're coming with us tonight."

Copernicus is back in town, so *prepare yourself* to rotate in a new direction.

In the ensuing commotion, Sylvia comes to my rescue like a fairy godmother. She stops the kidnappers from dragging me out of bed. She gets them out the door and into their car and off to a motel for the night. "Come back after breakfast," she tells them. Like normal people.

The next morning, when my bunk mates are choosing up

sides on the softball field, the yellow Chevy starts crawling up the camp road, slooooowly snaking around the tennis courts, past the infirmary, closing in on the pitcher's mound, where the camp owner, Sonny Golden, is standing tall beside me in his umpire's uniform, ready for them—his legs planted firmly apart, his whistle drawn, his hands on his hips in the Visiting Day equivalent of *High Noon*.

The Big Bang is bobbing out of the car window, screeching at him. "We're gonna shut this place down, Sonny."

My softball game grinds to a halt, and the tennis tournament has a mid-volley time-out while everyone assembles for Lola's guerilla theater. Nothing can compete with genuine hysteria.

Mort, chauffeur and warden, is doing his best to pull her back in the car and crank her window up. But she keeps rolling it down again, her head popping in and out like a jack-in-the-box, with big red hair and bee-stung lips and round turquoise patches of eye shadow. She looks like a carnival.

"We're gonna sue your pants off, Sonny."

Sonny blows his whistle and signals to Marsha Margaretten, the music counselor, to lead us in the camp anthem while he deals with the lunatic.

"*Under, thunder, bang and let it roll,*" we sing out.

"*Louder!*" Sonny roars.

Marsha waves her baton furiously, but we can't cover Lola. She's a showstopper.

Today, reprising the role of Salome, my mother wants the head of the nature counselor to be brought to her on a platter. Her performance—the whole shrieking, tearful turn of it—is even bigger than the one she gave last summer when I got back to our beach cottage from a walk in town with Ben and Helen. Narragansett was such a quaint village in the fifties that three children under nine could be allowed to find their way home alone, holding hands, stopping and looking both ways at every corner, just as they'd been taught. A powder blue sedan pulled up alongside us and stopped, with its motor running. The driver, a man of about thirty, slid over to the passenger's side and opened the door. "Hey, look at this," he said. Then he motioned for us to come closer. It may have been a cozy beach town, but I'd been warned about one thing: "Never take candy from a stranger." That was Lola-ism number one. Number two was "Protect your brother and sister." So I told Ben and Helen to walk home without me, and I, the eldest, marched bravely over to the blue car on my own, ready to refuse all offers, even if the man had Necco Wafers. Even if he had a whole roll of brown ones. When I was a foot away, he swung around on the seat to face me, and he pulled a crooked pink stick out of his pants. "Do you know what this is?" he asked. Frankly, I didn't have a clue. "It's a pee-pee," he said. And then he smiled. I stared at it, but it didn't resemble any pee-pee *I'd* ever seen. After a minute, he put the pink stick back in his pants, and he said "Thank you," and then he drove away. As the car turned the corner, he waved good-bye. No candy whatsoever was offered, and none was consumed, and so I proudly recounted the story when I got home. But Lola, always unpredictable, went berserk. She called Mort and the police and the fire department, and when they were all assembled in the tiny living room, she chewed up the scenery.

Judging from her stage turn at camp today, the man with the crooked pink pee-pee stick was small-time compared to the nature counselor, "Uncle" Artie, who must have been giving out candy like it was Halloween. Now, it appears, he's nowhere to be found.

Meanwhile, other children are being loaded into their families' cars, and a dusty caravan beats its way down the dirt road. Whether they're fleeing from Uncle Artie or Lola, or both, is anyone's guess.

Sonny is telling Lola to "be reasonable," which is both quaint and ludicrous, and after a while Mort gives up and drags her off to the car, ramming down the button to lock her in, as if that would do the trick, and then he runs around to his side and starts the ignition (Okay, everything's fine now.)

Ben and Helen are already in the backseat, with the windows up and their hands over their ears. Apparently, they're planning to brave it at home with Lola; maybe they think they can save her. But I am not so selfless. I'd rather take my chances here at camp with Uncle Artie.

A few days later, I get my only letter from home.

> *Dear Nancy,*
>
> *Everything is fine here. Mom gets better every day. When you get home from camp, she'll be waiting for you.*
>
> *Love,*
> *Dad*

That night, and for many nights thereafter, I dream I'm in the backseat of a car with two people; there are two more people up front. We're going around and around and around a dimly lit multilevel garage, looking for the exit. Most nights, the car goes around and *down*. Sometimes, it goes around and *up*. But it never stops going in circles. I have a feeling that if I were to stumble upon an exit and escape from this endless regression, I would still be where I started out—in my incongruously named hometown of Providence.

Which is why, when I was still having that dream in my thirties, I got behind the wheel of the car and drove it the hell out of that dark garage and moved to the City of Light.

TWO

Slouching Towards Providence

"*Quelle catastrophe!*" my boss says when I tell him I'm catching the next flight to the States, his comment ostensibly directed at my family tragedy, but more likely at the work he'll face at this seminal moment in our antiperspirant crusade. Between his lingering morning *promenade* and his premature bottle of *rouge* at lunch, Claude is in the office but an hour, barely enough time to put ink in his *plume*. This explains why he asked the home office to dispatch an American lackey *(moi)* to pick up the slack.

What's wrong with the French started long before Proust, long before he remembered everything after inhaling the madeleine. The problem started with Descartes—*I think, therefore I am* was the great-granddaddy of procrastination. Why do anything at all when the very act of thinking is so delightfully self-affirming? Four hundred years later, it's impossible to distinguish enlightenment from sloth. The taxi that takes me to Charles de Gaulle Airport is a claustrophobic Renault, which, like its driver, reeks of stale Gauloises and cut-rate cologne ladled on like vinaigrette. This is my target market, the great unwashed *Français*, and yet the tattered book that lies open on his front seat, beneath his massive slobbering sheepdog, is *Rules for the Direction of the Mind*, which Descartes began in 1627 and, tellingly, never completed.

Waiting for me at the gate is my friend Margot, whose own father died in a bizarre water accident when she was five. When he slipped in his bath, she tells me, he grabbed the nearest thing to break his fall, but unfortunately he grabbed the ceiling fixture, which was on, and his feet were still in the water. How he could have reached the ceiling if he was slipping is beyond me. If he was anything like *my* father, he probably stood up in his bath to change the bulb.

Margot is a chic, wiry woman who anticipates disaster everywhere and whose jittery movements and matching fluttering accessories bring the profile "high-strung" to life. In airports, this fidgeting makes her look like a drug dealer, and because of the ensuing embarrassment and occasional strip search, she's used to being upgraded to first class, where her flammable attitude can be segregated. She thinks I deserve an upgrade, too, for my pain and suffering, now that I'm a member of the Dead Father's Club.

"Tell the cabin crew you're on your way to your father's funeral, and they'll upgrade you. Tell them you might even be an *orphan*." This is the kind of thinking that makes her a great marketer.

Nevertheless, the stewardess thinks I'm demented when I deliver the pitch, as though my tragedy somehow entitles me to a wider seat, a tablecloth, a better Bordeaux. "*Dingue*," she keeps saying to the other flight attendants. "Nutcase." So I slouch into my assigned middle seat in the rear, ricocheting between heartbreak and humiliation, longing to be a more dignified person.

There's a proof of the relativity of time on airplanes, not just a metaphor about boredom and crossing datelines, but the real Einstein McCoy. Measured time slows down if a plane flies high enough and long enough, and on the trip to Providence, I am not just between two times zones but outside of both. The stewardess I tangled with ignores me ostentatiously, while the hazy glare of spooky light streams through the windows. Later, while everyone else is watching the latest Deneuve, I'm in a dark cavern with flickering images, where I see only my own home movie: his and hers coffins on a slow-motion conveyor belt, being lowered into the ground to a sound track of wailing in Hebrew.

From the duty-free cart, I buy a red Hermès scarf and an ounce of Shalimar for my comatose mother. Effusive shopping has always been the first whiff of her mania. Electric toothbrushes and WaterPiks, Waring blenders and Tupperware, Wedgwood china and Rosenthal stemware, a bigger TV set—better yet, make that two TV sets. The Fuller Brush man bumped into the Avon lady while our *Encyclopaedia Britannica* was being delivered.

Slinking home after school when I'm eight, a short, awkward, gap-toothed third grader, I hear the living room stereo blaring "Makin' Whoopee."

Picture a little love nest
Down where the roses cling . . .

Lola is stationed in the upstairs hallway, a twenty-eight-year-old curvy auburn tornado, aerobically jettisoning every loose object within reach. Turning the landing into a giant Dumpster to make room for "upgrades." Down with the shower curtains and off with the showerheads. Her generator is revved up so hot, there's an aura around her, of heat and static, a buzz I figure everyone can hear, and it makes my skin vibrate if I get too close. I am already in therapy, having been sent to the school doctor in first grade with my drawing of a shopping bag filled with mommies and daddies, all of whom were anatomically correct, except that the mommies were missing their heads.

Crossing Lola's debris pile, I trip over my sister's poodle skirt and cat's-eye glasses, my brother's toy doctor kit, and my stuffed penguin, Penny. She's the only plush toy I have left without surgical scars, since Ben has operated on all the others with his round-tipped scissors and hotel sewing kit, resetting their paws and repairing their hernias, then dousing the stitches in Mercurochrome. Doing unto the animals what has already been done unto him. Maybe a little more. "I need Penny," I cry, disappearing into my little cave, hiding under the covers with my transitional object, failing to transition, until my father calls us down to dinner.

The phone has been ringing, a sign we will have dunning with dinner. Mort's business, an insolvent brass factory fueled by delusions and insomnia, manufactures his "inventions." Like Bobby Pin Genie, a small brass compact with a magnet that, according to Lola's brochure, will attract and hold "all the bobby pins a woman could ever want." Or Finesse, "a lighter so slim, it fits inside a cigarette pack," with enough fluid to light about five cigarettes, so if the buyer doesn't mind carrying a pint refill of Ronson in his other pocket, it's perfect. "This is going to make us rich," Mort announced the night he brought home the sample, and I watched Lola start spending his money in her head, as though he were Thomas Edison and Finesse were General Electric.

It turned out that the world was not exactly waiting for Finesse, but in case the need ever picked up, Mort stored a thousand of them in a warehouse. Then he went out to the driveway, where he was happily up to his elbows in carburetors.

"Is the deadbeat at home?" the caller asks when I answer the phone, and I pass it to my father without hesitation, as though Deadbeat is his middle name.

Lola is wearing a jaunty new green apron, broiling steak and stirring milk and butter into mashed potatoes. If only Norman Rockwell could be here to paint us.

Meanwhile, beads of sweat pop up on Mort's face like heat blisters, and he looks like he's going to blow. "Go ahead and sue me," he yells into the phone, trying to get out from under Lola's latest acquisitions—subscriptions to the Book of the Month Club and *Reader's Digest* and *The Atlantic Monthly* and eighteen other assorted periodicals that she ordered for five years, the day after he brought home Finesse.

But this night is different from all other nights. Why? Because on this night, before Mort hangs up on the bill collector, he improvises a cocky remark: "I'll just tell the judge she's crazy."

Although I think it all the time, *crazy* is not a word my family says out loud, not even to one another. "Crazy" is our secret.

My steak is leeching puddles of red fat onto my untouched plate when Lola grabs hers, dumps its contents and her silverware into the garbage disposal, and lets it rip. Then she pulls a mangled butter knife out of the sink and points it at Mort.

"You can't say that. I won't let you."

"Cut it out," he orders, as if *he* could control *her*, when she's already *lunging* at him, discharging electricity like a downed power line.

Mort jumps up so fast, he knocks the table over, and my steak and potatoes, which I am always so careful to keep separated on my plate, hit the floor in a mosaic of Fiestaware and A1 sauce. I suck the last bit of oxygen out of the air, wondering if the cutlery will wind up in the dishwasher or Mort's heart. He shields himself behind the table, our knight in red Formica armor, the chrome legs thrust out like sabers. I, less brave, crouch behind a wall around the corner. Lola has the only view of everybody, and she's still moving with the knife in her hand.

I squint into the half-life of that moment, trying to sharpen the fuzzy image, to bring what's blurry into focus. Does sharpening a fuzzy image make it clearer, or further distort it? Memory is slippery, and the closer I get to the bottom of it, the less traction there is. How did Mort wind up on his back on the floor with the knife in *his* hand? How did the blood get on his shirt? And whose blood is it? True, the weapon was last seen in Lola's hand, and she seemed ready to plunge it through his heart, but she might have dropped it, or changed her mind and thrown it on the floor. And conceivably, Mort could have fallen on it by mistake, or even stabbed himself to make a point. Who knows? *Who knows?* Is it enough evidence to convict?

After the climax, Ben, who is six, runs to his room and blares Strauss—a scratchy recording of *Elektra,* which he plays over and over on his toy Victrola like a theme song. It's an extended mad scene in which the famous mezzo Jean Madeira puts an operatic sheen on what we've just witnessed downstairs. A few bars of anguish, a heartbreaking high note, then the blood is spilled.

When the opera ends, Ben throws my pet bunny down the cellar stairs in a medical experiment "to see if it will die." It does.

I raise the heat on his aquarium. Good-bye, guppies.

Helen builds a toothpick launching pad for Lola's Tampax in the living room bay window, where she uses her own urine as jet fuel and sets fire to the string.

We all tell on one another.

. . .

Later that night, our parents' energetic reconciliation wakes me, as it often does, since they copulate with the frequency of fruit flies, and perhaps because they like an audience, they don't lock their bedroom door.

I walked in on them accidentally the first time when I was five. I tried to pretend I wasn't horrified and excited in some strange new way by watching my naked father roll over on top of my naked mother and then roll her back on top of him—even then it seemed like more rolling than necessary under the circumstances—their naked buttocks flipping by like flash cards.

I walked right past them that first night and held my head high, as though I'd seen that sort of thing a million times before, being five, and I got whatever stupid toy I'd barged in for while they lay in bed giggling, *tittering,* without bothering to pull up the sheets.

The second time was just a few nights later, and the house was so quiet that I thought they might be asleep. Maybe I'd had a nightmare, or maybe I was investigating; I don't know. Their door was unlocked, of course, no lessons having been learned from my first intrusion, and when I barged in, there was an instant replay of the previous episode: their triple-axel buttocks-flipping and my insouciance. But this time, I was glued to their performance, absorbed and repelled by the spectacle, turned off and turned on. I have no idea how many more of these installments I participated in, but years later a psychiatrist, who wasn't trying to be clever, said I was repressing "penis and vagina shock." How bad is that? I wondered but didn't ask. When does it end?

Helen's preschool output consisted of small clay figures with jumbo genitalia—mostly stallions with huge phalluses. For our birthdays, she made Ben a penis pencil holder and me a vagina vase.

So I was hardly the only one.

Sometimes the feeling in a home is palpable—a buzz you don't need a sixth sense for. Our home was orgasmic. If there was sex going on in my friends' houses, it was handled in a dignified fashion behind locked doors. But at our house, it was out there. Providence was a lot like Mayberry in the fifties, but Lola wasn't exactly Aunt Bee.

On the night of the butter knifing, rather than bursting into their room, I content myself with eavesdropping, lying on the floor in the hall, my ear to the crack under their door—ready to intervene at the first sound of attempted homicide. But both of them are braying like bullfrogs, as usual, with the mattress springs croaking in counterpoint. As a murder weapon, the butter knife was a failure, but as foreplay, it was a huge success.

Then something I can't quite hear, something she's whispering, makes the galloping mattress slow to a trot.

"No," I hear her say. "Don't."

I would have squeezed under the door if I could have.

"*Stop* it."

There's a heavy thud, as though a body has fallen—or been pushed—to the floor. Then footsteps. Their bathroom door opens and slams shut. The bolt turns.

"That's enough," she says from behind the door. "I'm not licking all of it."

Licking it? Licking *what*?

Mort is silent.

"Bill made me lick it all."

Who the hell is *Bill*? And what did *he* give her to lick?

"Enough already with Bill," Mort says. "Bill was twenty years ago."

. . .

By the time I get up the next morning, Lola is sprawled out on the living room carpet, still in her pink nightgown, facedown and wailing. Mort isn't even trying to get her back to bed, but her mother, our savior, has arrived.

Nana is a short, zaftig marshmallow with warm jelly arms and soft almond eyes. Her eyebrows are like Claudette Colbert's, two perfect circumflexes, the last vestige of her legendary showgirl looks. In her twenties, her name was "up in lights on Broadway, in BIG letters," or so she loves to tell me before lifting her housedress to reveal her assets. "The Girl with the Million Dollar Legs" tap-danced with Jimmy Durante and Eddie Cantor. But her legs have since grown pudgy, and now they operate a foot press at the rubber factory in Pawtucket, where she works the graveyard shift so she can take care of us on days when Lola is "under too much pressure." Like today.

Lola wants the truth about Bill, which I'd like, too, and she's been pounding the carpet as though she can beat the secret out of it. She certainly hasn't been able to beat anything out of Nana so far, and I can't even figure out the connection.

"Nothing happened," Nana says over and over again, unwavering. Weeping. "Nothing happened. Don't cry."

But Lola doesn't stop crying.

"Nothing happened, Lola—the doctor said the cherry wasn't broken."

So now I know the flavor.

When things were spinning out of control, when the center of the universe was wobbly in her trajectory, whenever Bill came up, three things happened in quick succession: My grandmother moved in, my mother ran away to the temple, and my father ran after her. I can't figure out how my mother managed to escape from the house once Nana was installed in the living room—

like the guardian at the gates of hell—but Lola could get the car down the driveway before anyone was onto her.

By the time Mort realizes she's missing that morning, our Chevy is already turning the corner and heading south on Elmgrove Avenue. He commandeers my little Schwinn and I follow on a tricycle, each of us folded in half, our knees grazing our shoulders, like clowns. Bringing up the rear is Alice, our howling beagle, who cuts Mort off on Sessions Street, sending him headfirst over the handlebars and onto the sidewalk, with the bike on top of him, its wheel spinning a nasty piece of beagle ear in a circle of blood that looks like some awful Pollock drip painting.

Nana catches up on foot. "The ear'll grow back. Don't you worry," she tells me when she sees the carnage. She has a knack for saying just the right thing.

We are not religious people—twice a year to temple for the High Holy Days is our limit—but the temple is where my mother runs for comfort when she's in high astronomical gear. There she communes with the spirit of her grandfather, the late, great Rabbi Bachrach, a renowned teacher of kabbalah, who taught her the "sacred mysteries" and the path to the "invisible world"—where he now resides permanently and where she occasionally visits him.

My father and I sprint through the old wing of the hugest temple in town, through its narrow, creaky hallways, past a decrepit pulpit, where I'm sure there's a dead body in a coffin, to a dark cavern in the back, which is the junior rabbi's musty study. Smells of mold and candle wax halt me in the doorway, although Mort rushes right in.

Lola is sitting across from the dumbstruck young rabbi, speed-talking in her special language, mathspeak, bandying polynomials about, calculating *pi* and *phi*, breathless to the *nth*. Infinity is calling.

Rabbi Schulman is a *junior* rabbi, still on training wheels, and Lola is giving him a test drive.

"Zero, one, one, two, three, five, eight," Lola says, teasing him with a beginner's Fibonacci. Even my little sister knows the next number is the sum of the previous two.

"Thirteen," he coughs up after a pause.

Lola fires off a brisk barrage. "Twenty-one, thirty-four, fifty-five, eighty-nine, one forty-four, two thirty-three, three seventy-seven . . ."

I know where she's headed but cannot keep up. And why would I want to? Lola believes if you connect with the numbers in just the right way, God flows right through you. I say no thanks.

After the math lesson, she moves on to her riddles of the Old Testament.

"The golden mean / Divides the sea / Religious opportunity."

She winks at the rabbi, giving him a minute to answer, but he doesn't seem to realize she's asked a question.

And before I can say "Passover," she collapses.

Thoughts are supposed to flow through the brain like canoes on a calm lake. Every so often, they come to a portage and have to make their way across. If you're wired right, these little canoes get transported by a chemical shuttle and are hospitably received on the other side, where they continue their voyage until they deliver their message. But if you're wired wrong, they run aground, or, worse, they capsize in the swirling crosscurrent, and sometimes they get sucked into the undertow. Imagine these thought vessels up a mental creek without a neurological paddle, plunging over the edge of a psychological precipice and spilling into the deluge. My mother's family struggled in this headwater for generations. It was their biochemical itinerary.

I know now that Aunt Flossie's symptoms were first called

"the vapors." For Aunt Lily, it was "neurasthenia." Aunt Annie was a "dipsomaniac." Such polite, romantic terms, a tale of emerging vocabulary and cultural explanation, and our family tree evolved along with the psychiatric diagnostic manual.

Hypochondria, hallucination, hysteria.

Neuritis, neuralgia, neurosis.

"She's just been under too much pressure is all," my father explains, but the rabbi calls an ambulance, and the rest is medical history.

Ben and Helen were at our temple Hebrew school that day, but before the ambulance arrived, the rabbi evacuated the premises—so they missed seeing Lola get carried out in a straitjacket. She was taken to Shady Tree Sanitarium, the best private psychiatric facility in the state, much better than the public asylum where Lily and Annie and Flossie were sent—where their shrink was a suicide.

At Shady Tree, Lola got the treatment du jour—a Nembutal-induced "sleep cure." But a week later, when my mother awakened from her beauty rest with hallucinations, when she still heard voices calling her name, when she accused the doctors of changing their identities, they brought out the second course: intravenous barbiturates. Later, the antipsychotic agents were called in—hard-edged drugs that made her stiff-legged and dull-eyed and thick-brained. And when that didn't suffice, it was time for the psychiatric equivalent of the nuclear bomb—shock treatment.

"They put a rain hat on my head, with an elastic around it," she told me. "I went into a room and jumped up on a table. Then they told me to lie down, and that's all I remember."

After she lay down, they used restraints to tie her arms and legs to the table, attached electrodes to her rain hat, and clamped a bite stick between her teeth. Then they got the hell out of the way. What followed was a high-voltage shower, spraying twenty joules into her rain bonnet, zapping her with five thousand times the electrical wattage of the brain—without a surge protector—until she convulsed. They fairly made her hum. Electroconvulsive therapy is the only approved treatment that, used as directed, induces epilepsy, amnesia, and apathy, in that order.

That certainly calmed her down for a while.

Bill and the cherry were extinguished, temporarily anyway, but plenty of her other memories were collateral damage. And there were no more math tricks.

"Unfortunate side effect," her doctor told Mort, "but not unanticipated."

After all, the little shower cap was a one-size-fits-all model, and the best map of the brain in the fifties was as fuzzy as America before Columbus. Hard to pinpoint where a cherry would put down roots, but probably somewhere up front. Whole chunks of Lola were scorched earth, and for long stretches of time, she couldn't remember my birthday or our phone number or the business potential of Bobby Pin Genie. Or whether she'd had an affair with Max or just imagined it.

During her static period, she sent me up the block to Doyle's, the apothecary on Hope Street, to run an urgent errand for her. For that mission, at eight years old, I was entrusted with a five-dollar bill, and when I walked into the store, breathless from running uphill, I threw wide the front door with the authority of a sheriff bursting into a saloon and knocked down a display. It was dark inside, and the three old men sipping coffee at the counter weren't visible until my eyes adjusted, but by then I'd already announced my mission.

"I'm here for Kotex," I proclaimed, broadcasting what I'd rehearsed on the way, "And don't forget a Kotex belt."

Then I noticed the men.

"Six Kotex or twelve Kotex?" Mr. Doyle yelled from the back. "Light flow or heavy?"

How did I answer? How did I quantify my mother's menstrual flow? Did I get change back from her five-dollar bill? The memory is a long skid mark. I crept out of Doyle's and never went back. Over time, a few months, Lola's brownout began to lift and she went back to buying her own sanitary pads.

She graduated from gluing seashells onto cigar boxes to spending hours at the piano, picking out chords from her fake books and belting along.

Today, "Cry Me a River."

Tomorrow, "Happy Days Are Here Again."

Soon enough, her electricity came all the way back on, and when she was fully charged, she turned on her floodlights and became the life of the party once more. And for a while, until another overload tripped her circuit breakers, she lit up the sky all over again.

In college, when I read Heisenberg (okay, maybe I read the Cliffs Notes version), I didn't grasp the concept of uncertainty until I thought about Lola. You can determine a particle's speed or its direction, but not both simultaneously, so even if you know how fast it's moving, you can't know where it will wind up or when it will get there. This was familiar. Lola traveled at the speed of light, but I never knew where she was headed or when she would arrive, and every one of her appearances was unpredictable. Lola was unknowable. And to hear her tell it, she might be from an alternate universe. So I didn't call her Mommy; I called her Mommy *Hornstein*, as though I had a saner, secret Mommy hidden somewhere else, in a better nuclear family, under a different last name.

She stood too close to me one day at the bathroom sink,

staring into my mirror, in my too-small bathroom in my tiny apartment in my claustrophobic life at graduate school. That was ten years ago. What made her squeeze into the bathroom with me? The space wasn't big enough for both of us and I was there first, but she pushed her way in and stood at my side, so close that I could feel the heat of her, smearing on her red lipstick while I washed my face. When I raised my eyes, she was looking straight at me in the mirror, moving the brassy lipstick tube around and around and around her thick red lips; it was dizzying, and she seemed to be coming from someplace inside me, someplace I knew she shouldn't be. I was backstage, in the wings of my own life, watching her in the center ring, hypnotized. And just like that, I disappeared into her. I was sucked right into the mirror, through her lips and into the abyss.

After that, I doodled red lips for years. Abstract lips and expressionist lips and runny lips that dripped like Dalí clocks. Headless lips the size of an Oldenburg sculpture.

I had to push my way out of the bathroom that day, had to crawl around my mother to get away from her and catch my breath. I didn't ask her why she'd driven fifty miles to see me—there'd certainly been no invitation. But when she was finally back in her white mink coat and ready to leave, when the engine was running in her new blue Buick Electra with its LOLA vanity plates, she lowered her window, and she confessed.

"I'm not feeling quite myself."

Just that simple sentence.

And I knew it was going to happen again.

"What do you mean?" I asked, pretending I'd misunderstood, that maybe she didn't mean to sound so ominous.

"I just don't feel quite right. You know," she said, tapping the side of her head, "my thinking."

I knew what she meant, but I asked anyway. "Your *thinking*?"

"It's like Aunt Flossie's taking over my thinking again."

There they were. The awful magic words. The incantation. The invocation of Aunt Flossie, who was not just *meshuggah*. Aunt Flossie was certifiable.

Cue the ambulance; warm up the electric rain hat.

Lola's medical history reads like the chapter headings of a psychiatric manual. "Too much pressure" made things implode and explode, one big bang after another, throwing our family into the air, too high, sinking feeling, no net. It started before I was old enough to make sense of things, and it's the chaos out of which my own sense of things is made. The raw material of my memory is a long, slow stew in her Crock-Pot, rich in bite and piquancy and full of sinew. Maybe her DNA was twisted too tight in the first place, but when Bill made her lick it all, whether or not he broke her cherry, he broke *her*.

After Nana died, I learned who Bill was—her obituary listed him as her first husband, which made him, I assumed, Lola's father. Cousin Izzy, who's Lola's age, put it together for me. He said Bill left town abruptly when they were five, and although no one said why at the time, Izzy knew. One day, when he was alone at home, studying in his room, Uncle Bill came in and sat down on the edge of his bed and told him to scoot over and read out loud. Izzy was still on the first page when his left hand felt a hard, wet thing, and before he got to the end of the chapter, Izzy had to lick it all, too.

The flight from Paris turns turbulent over the ocean, and although I've never had any trouble sleeping on planes, when I do, I generally dream that the plane is crashing. Every bump is a nosedive straight into the abyss, and my vigilant startle response is all that keeps the plane aloft. Experts tell me this is due to a fear of losing control. (Thank you very much.)

Trapped in an aluminum bucket just a few inches thicker

than Reynolds Wrap, hurtling through space with nothing but my worst fears for company, I am trying not to fall asleep. And not to dwell on Sunny von Bülow.

I tighten my seat belt, lean back in my middle seat in economy, and attempt to pray. My fear of flying is long-standing, but this will be my first resort to prayer, since my lifelong religious views fall into the category of utter disbelief. But this is a special occasion. A life hangs in the balance, and I don't mean my own, so if there is a god and I fail to pray, will someone be punished for my sin of omission? My mother? The odds (and the guilt) are enough to test my atheism. If there is a god, maybe my prayer will be answered; and if there isn't a god, what do I have to lose, except maybe a little more self-respect?

But where to begin? Whom to address? Yahweh is out of the question—so wrathful and male—and he has that awful slogan, "I am that I am," which reminds me of Popeye. I prefer a lowercase god, gender-neutral, powerful but not conceited. And definitely not vengeful.

Dear god. Are you there? ARE YOU LISTENING? And can you take my call?

I'm calling collect after all these years of not giving you so much as a passing thought, and I feel pretty sleazy about that. But of course you must already know what I'm thinking, since you see us when we're sleeping, and you know when we're awake. I'm sorry I called you a pyramid scheme. In the future, though, you'll see. You'll be at the top of my to-do list. The sky's the limit, if you'll just front me a little credit right now. Anything you're comfortable giving under the circumstances. Maybe get me home before my mother dies? Or consider calling off the double funeral? Would it be possible to wake Lola up, rested and refreshed, like Sleeping Beauty? And with absolutely no brain damage, please, god? Would that be doable?

I hold my breath, expecting nothing. There's no thunderbolt, which is a good thing, since the plane is at thirty thousand feet, but it leaves my fundamental questions unanswered: Is there a deity, anthropomorphic or otherwise, with or without an intelligent design, benevolent or angry, responsible or irresponsible, but nevertheless in charge?

Is god up there listening, but not interested in helping? Or would he like to help but he's unable to intervene? Which is worse? Does it matter?

Maybe god means well and had what it took to get the world started, but things have spun out of control. Maybe he's in over his head—like the Peter Principle. Maybe he's still as powerful as he ever was, but he can't figure out what to do. The old bean may not be as robust as it once was, so he forgets things and loses track of details. Now big streams of life flow unchecked, and others go right down the drain. Maybe he confuses people, or starts projects he loses interest in, or maybe he can't remember where he left off. Or maybe it's worse: God could be powerless *and* forgetful, impotent as well as obtuse; tired and grumpy and disinterested. God could be at the end of his rope, like so many of us. And sick of being used.

Or maybe he likes the world this way—dangerous and messy and unpredictable. I say there's a good chance god is up there on his infinite practice tee, gripping the handle of his long, hard driver, and he's been banging away at a bottomless bucket of balls for eternity.

Doesn't he know it's chaos down here? I say judge him by his effects. Hold him accountable.

And so I fail to pray.

With connections, the trip to Providence takes all day, and I doze off on the last leg. In my dream, I am a candy striper. An old woman lying in a hospital bed hands me a newspaper. *Read me this story*, she says, but when I look at it, the paper is blank. In walks a nun, who takes the paper out of my hand, and *she* can read it with no trouble. The woman in bed, smiling, hands me an old timepiece. *Tell me the time*, she says. But the clock has no hands.

I wake up in a time capsule as we're landing, hovering above my destination, with no perspective on it, while my father is being autopsied or embalmed, or both, and my mother is comatose, or worse. Everyone knows that death makes time run out. It's "no parenthesis," as Cummings said. But an accident that's still flirting with death lacks final punctuation—it's a hyphen that could tip either way.

I like to pretend that locking the doors and stocking the cupboards will protect me from the boogeyman. I double-knot my shoelaces and never let my gas tank fall below half. But *Semper Paratus* is no match for the haphazard tyranny of an accident, for its unexpected punch to the soft underbelly of happiness.

"I'm dead, aren't I?" my mother asked me years ago, apropos of nothing, while gluing seashells to a cigar box after a round of shock. "You're just not telling me the truth yet, huh?"

THREE

Intimations of Mortality

The plastic bubble of Charles de Gaulle Airport, with its octopus pods and hallucinogenic walkways, bears no resemblance to the one-room terminal outside of Providence, where my plane has to stop short of the gate while a gangplank is towed up to retrieve the passengers. From a distance, I spot Helen, my younger sister, using sign language I can't comprehend—two fingers and a thumb bobbing along, bobbing along, with a wrist-swishing coda. A psychologist specializing in the deaf, she's come a long way since my mother told her to stop talking with her hands. Not until I am thirty feet away can I see her mouth is as wide as Joe E. Brown's, miming the words *NO CHANGE*. Then she smiles. The smile is supposed to mean this is good news, or she is courageous, or I should buck up, or all of the above.

Helen is a beauty, with Lola's curly red hair and a twinkle in her green eyes, and she's wearing the buttery leather pants I bought myself in Saint-Germain but could never squeeze into. Psychotherapist, professor, department chair, author (and yogini in her spare time), she's put the manageable amount of mania we all inherited to good use, piling on the serial successes to prove she wasn't just "an accident."

Lola believed, and often said, that I was "the smart one" and Benny was "the musical one"—as though we were brands or Platonic Forms. Ben was so cowed by the notion that I owned *smart* that he nearly failed first grade. While he was failing second grade, Lola had his IQ tested and then began telling him *he* was the smart one (and her favorite). And after that, he got straight A's and eventually graduated summa.

Alas, the third child, poor Helen, was born after the roles of "smart" and "musical" were already cast and had to create a new identity from scratch. There were few resources to advise her—Ben and I were already consumed with our own neuroses, and our parents had *real* problems. A brief flirtation with guitar confirmed her unmusicalness, and *smartness* was reserved and had a backup. *Who*, then, to be?

Probably not by nature, but certainly by default, Helen turned into "the wild child" and earned the nickname "Hellish." She traveled with as fast a crowd as a six-year-old could find in the fifties on the Jewish East Side of Providence. Repeatedly confined to her room for small and large transgressions, she learned how to climb out her window and slide down the drainpipe. She was often on the lam and became a precocious thief. But the only place she stole from was the little library on Rochambeau Avenue, and from there she pilfered only poetry.

"You can't have a library card without your mother's signature," the librarian had said, scolding her. At the time, Lola was in Shady Tree and not giving autographs. So Helen had to sneak into the library. She waited outside until a group headed up the steps, then ran in along with them and hid in the poetry corner, which was not visible from the main desk. From those dwindling shelves she filched a book a month—a six-year-old hiding Walt Whitman under her yellow slicker. Poetry was all she was able to understand on the main floor shelves, and no one had bothered to tell her there was a children's section upstairs.

A year into it, by then a Chaucer specialist, she got caught when an Illustrated copy of *Canterbury Tales* fell out of her skimpy T-shirt at the door. It didn't seem like a well-planned heist to me or to Ben, who was a bit of an expert in these matters and practiced his own larceny at the nearby drugstore. Helen should have worn a jacket, he said. And why didn't she just forge her library card in the first place, as he would have?

Her shrink insisted that she wanted to get caught, but by then I knew shrinks would say anything to cover up for not figuring things out themselves. The Helen Hornstein Poetry Library was unearthed beneath her bed—she'd stashed away Emily Dickinson and Robert Frost like pornography magazines.

Small wonder, then, that it wasn't until she got to college (read: out of the house) that Helen began to bloom. She majored in abnormal psych, which felt just like home to her, and discovered she could paint and sculpt. Somehow, she merged the fields and wound up with a doctorate in art therapy. Helen is the only psychologist I know with a throw wheel in her office and a kiln in her basement.

The agenda she's organized for tomorrow, Memorial Day, begins with Mort's funeral at ten, with equal odds he'll be accompanied. The twin coffins continue their slow procession to the graveside in my mind. Meanwhile, Ben is still installed at the "little Catholic hospital" he bemoaned, trying to increase Lola's chances in intensive care, where we are discouraged from visiting.

The phrase "life support" is used repeatedly.

References to God are made.

Helen takes the highway in Mort's secondhand gold Caddy, which once gave me a bogus sense of his success but now wails from both ends, its fan belt whining under the hood and its muffler hacking in the rear. An odor of burning carcinogens accompanies us, and when we arrive, I need a crowbar to pry my braised suitcase from the trunk. Helen inspects the Caddy's engine with great authority, having spent her childhood at our father's side in the driveway, "repairing" things. Her investigation reveals that "someone" has removed the catalytic converter, enabling the car to use cheaper, leaded gas, but the consequence is enough heat to corrode the muffler and melt Samsonite.

My father's nickname, I don't need to be reminded, is "Mr. Fix It." The boat is his namesake, and he took her apart and put her back together a little at a time, in the order in which it was necessary, patching her parts and jerry-rigging what he couldn't repair.

My parents' downsized apartment in Cranston, where they moved after our wobbly nest in Providence emptied out, is a split-level, with steps every fourteen feet clotting the main arteries—up to the kitchen, down to the den—so going from room to room feels like limping. The pullout couch I'm to sleep on is parked next to a shin-splitting glass coffee table on a beige shag rug, amid "wood paneling" that wouldn't give a splinter even if humped naked. There's no place like home.

With its floral-themed walls—Marimekko poppies in the kitchen and flocked fleurs-de-lis in the bedroom—the apartment is decorated like a terrarium, and tonight, funereal bouquets bloom on every surface. Huge arrangements have been sent by friends, family, and the charities that have been outlets for Lola's relentless energy and boundless goodwill. She's been a drama coach at the Hebrew school, a play lady at the Children's Hospital, president of the PTA, president of the Home for the

Aged, president of the Brandeis Women's Committee, founder of the Paraplegic Association, and charter member of the governor's commission on the handicapped. The condolence cards are vague, taking no position on the names or number of victims, since it isn't yet clear who will be left standing in the morning.

I prepare myself to be the recipient of all this good cheer by pouring vodka straight up. Unbeatable in speed to glass, incomparable in rapidity of onset. A second dose will ensure the longevity of effect. Betty Ford will have to wait.

"*L'Chaim,*" I say to Helen as the kitchen door opens and Ben walks in. Nicknamed "Dr. Pecs" for his robust physique, my handsome, clean-cut, buttoned-down brother looks haggard and hasn't slept or shaved in days.

Then the postmortem begins.

Mort's cabin cruiser, the *Mr. Fix It,* had never left the dock the day he died. The year before, when it nearly capsized in the ocean off Martha's Vineyard, the deal Lola made with God was this: If they made it back to Folly's Landing, the boat would stay in its slip until all of the nautical niceties were in order. Spending the night at the dock would be the extent of her risk, although even that turned out to be too much. Not all boats are safe in their harbor.

The exhaust from the generator baked and smoked them all night through, churning out poison-packed heat for about eighteen hours before anyone at the yacht club noticed. By the time Mort was dragged from his berth, he'd been dead so many hours, his body was in rigor mortis—at least a dozen hours, Ben says knowingly. How did we ever get along before autopsy reports?

Lola, who lay beside him, was in a deep coma, but she still had a pulse. A doctor on a nearby boat rushed over with a canister of oxygen and kept her alive while his wife called an ambulance and a dozen onlookers screamed helplessly for more help.

Part of the protocol for carbon-monoxide poisoning is lowering the body temperature in a hyperbaric chamber with chilled superoxygenated air. Lola, however, stewed in the equatorial heat of the boat, then lay on the dock under the afternoon sun as a well-meaning deckhand covered her with a blanket so she wouldn't "catch her death of cold."

Before the ambulance arrived, she failed the neurological preliminaries—the clonus, the Hoffman, and the Babinski. There was no motor response, not even to pain. No speech, not even groaning. And no change in pupil size, not even with a bright light. Nothing in, nothing out. It's an ancient philosophical axiom that from nothing, nothing can come.

Ben learned about the accident when he got back to his apartment in Manhattan that afternoon, after his sleepless overnight shift at Bellevue. An unfamiliar voice on his answering machine announced that his mother was in a little hospital he'd never heard of in a beach town he'd never been to called Wakefield. His father—suspiciously—wasn't mentioned.

Three hours later, after a commuter flight and then a drive through back roads to the ocean, Ben made it to Our Lady by the Sea, where the weekend ER staff was in chaos, with everyone shouting orders to prep the comatose patient for ambulance transfer to a "better" hospital. As though the choices fifty miles away in Providence were between Mount Sinai and the Mayo Clinic. As though the patient stood a chance of surviving a road trip.

Lola was a cherry red color Ben had seen only in textbooks, as if she'd spent the night steeping in pigment, and her blood chemistry was like exhaust from a tailpipe. A respirator pushed oxygen through the soot in her lungs, and her arms and legs were tied down so they wouldn't fracture during her seizures. The thrashing had stopped before he arrived, so now she looked mounted, as though she were being prepped for taxidermy.

"Was she brought in alone?" Ben asked.

"There's a guy in the morgue," he was told.

That was how my brother learned that our father was dead.

Then he got to work.

In the ER at Bellevue, trauma is the norm—severed limbs, gunshot wounds, circus acts gone awry—and Ben had been trained to work on autopilot, never thinking about outcomes, just *working*, working *faster*. No time for doubts that weren't his to have anyway; they were somebody else's. But at Our Lady by the Sea, with his father in a drawer nearby and his mother on the table in front of him, he couldn't find the neutral zone he was supposed to work in. The admitting physician, a seventy-year-old family doctor standing nervously beside him, had already written Lola off, noting in her chart that the patient was unlikely to survive her "comma."

Ben canceled her road trip. He'd heard enough stories about the white light at the end of the long tunnel to imagine Mort at the other end, beckoning Lola to come along, and a back-road ambulance ride would be just the ticket. But Ben had also had patients who'd found their way out of the tunnel and who'd come back to tell the story. After working Lola up for an hour, having exhausted every rational procedure, he placed his warm hands carefully on her forehead and used them to try to call her back.

"I know you can hear me, Mom."

"Your hands are vessels," Lola used to tell him as a child. "I hear voices coming through them." It was a statement that revealed as much about the speaker as it did about the subject.

"You have to try harder," he whispered. "You need every bit of energy you've got if you want to come back."

He'd gone to a play a few nights before, *K2*, about two climbers stranded in an avalanche in the Himalayas, freezing and delirious and smothering. One was injured and couldn't go on, and the other had to leave him, or stay and die, too. Ben stood over Lola, with his fingers talking through her temples, trying to convince her to leave Mort behind, after her life of doing just the opposite. They'd eloped as soon as Mort got out of the army, in 1945, when she was eighteen, and the deed got her expelled from a women's college in Vermont. *The road not taken*.

Thirty-eight years later, as she lay dying at the final fork in the road she'd willingly taken, Ben was by her side, whispering an alternate itinerary.

After a while, she twitched. It was just a twitch, Ben says. But a small spasm can be like a generator kicking in.

And now, he says, "Time will tell."

In most respects, my brother is a scientist, but when it comes to his hands, he's a magician, and although we are a family of skeptics, we all believe in his touch. Gloveless in winter, his fingers radiate heat. They're hardly beautiful, though, especially the curvy stump where his right thumb should be. Ben was born with three thumbs—a normal one on his left hand and something like a lobster claw on his right, and the doctors quickly whittled his eleven digits down to a more manageable nine and a half. For years, his thumb stump was treated to fanciful reconstruction—its center was pithed with a metal rod; its skin was filigreed with wire; and every centimeter was sealed with sutures—but despite the stitching and scaffolding, the stub remained crooked and wouldn't sprout a knuckle or a bone. Eventually, the doctors ran out of procedures; my parents had no more heart for the torture; and Ben, who had taken this beneficent surgical abuse in good humor, seemed not to care.

"So what," my three-year-old brother overheard the last of his surgeons say. "So he'll never be a concert pianist. So what."

"He won't be a surgeon, either," our father complained at the time—not to motivate Ben, although that's how it turned out, since he'd heard every word and had our mother's flair for defiance. Although his curvy thumb could never be made to straighten out, it provided plenty of direction for him and an early lesson in the erroneous nature of appearance for me.

One afternoon, before he could read, before he started first grade, Ben sat down at the piano in our living room, following my own talentless and unprepared lesson, and he played a Chopin waltz by ear. His little left hand could barely stretch an octave, and his right hand was limited by the reconstructed lobster claw, but his fingers moved across the keyboard with the grace of natural acrobats. The phrase "musical prodigy" was bandied about. And a few years later, around the time I was learning to multiply, he won his school science contest and was dubbed a "polymath." True, his first patient, the live bunny I brought home from a magic show, met an untimely death in his experiment "to see if it would die." But his musical experiments were entirely victimless and got rave reviews from the start.

By contrast, my own piano career was euthanized when I was twelve by Mrs. Rubenstein, my teacher, whose musical judgment was merciful, if not swift. In my fourth year with her, when I still hadn't mastered "Für Elise," she told me that lots of people stop music lessons prematurely and then regret it—but my quitting, she admitted, was overdue. And then she cut me loose.

"Sol Hurok came to the house when Ben was in first grade," Lola recounted a few years before the accident, in an impromptu story about our wunderkind. She'd been reading the *Providence Journal*, tapping her lacquered red nails on the kitchen table like ten Rockettes dancing on a Formica stage, when she noticed Hurok's photo in an ad.

"Wow, the famous Sol Hurok?" Ben asked.

"Yup, there's only one. The impresario," she said. "Sol discovered Ben. He was here in Providence, rehearsing a show downtown, something big at the Arena, and he heard about Ben's hands." The information flowed off her like electric current.

"So you took me to an audition?"

"I didn't have to. Sol phoned me and insisted on coming right over. I couldn't keep him away."

"And then?" Ben asked, pushing her for details.

"And so you played for him; you played the 'Minute Waltz.' You hit every note perfectly, as only a mother can attest, and since you were only six, Sol figured he'd discovered a Jewish Mozart. He begged me to let you tour with him, but you were too young. I turned him down."

She turned the page, and the Rockettes warmed up again.

While I had never doubted Ben's talent, none of us, including Ben, could actually remember the illustrious Sol Hurok being on a first-name basis with Lola and coming over to the house with contracts. And that's because she made the whole thing up. She saw Hurok's picture in the paper and said the first thing that came into her head, elaborating as she went along. That was what she always did: She lied.

She lied because she felt like it and because she was good at it. She lied about how much she paid for a dress, whether her jewelry was real, whether she really lost her bathing suit or just decided to swim in the nude, and especially which one of us she loved the most.

While most people are afraid of getting caught in a lie, my mother thought that the truth was a trap. Lies have latitude and longitude. A lie can be extended, magnified, hedged, contradicted, circumvented, and denied. The truth, on the other hand, is a forkless road with a dead end. "A little lie never hurt anybody" she'd say philosophically, waving her moral airbrush, and if we'd had a family crest, that would have been its inscription.

One sign of a whopper was the sparkle she'd get in her eye

when she was at the beginning of a good one, a story with legs. But the sparkle wasn't a foolproof indicator, since she also gleamed when she'd had a few, or when she'd done something she didn't want to talk about at all, or when a couple of days went by after she'd stopped taking her lithium.

Then the poems and jingles began, with their dizzying leaps between tenuously connected subjects, words linked by rhyme but not by meaning and laid out in couplets. Her obsession with meter is what one expert called "metromania," a condition it's hard to believe there's a clinical name for. What my father lovingly called her "poetic license" was diagnosed as pseudologia-phantastica (aka pathological exaggeration). Their "yacht," according to my mother, is fifty feet (subtract twenty-three), with "a luxurious galley" (strike *luxurious*), and what she dubbed "the stateroom" is a blueprint for claustrophobia, where only a midget could stand (a dank crypt even when it isn't filling up with poison gas).

After the Mort postmortem, I leave my siblings in the kitchen to go warm up Mort's steam bath, one of the many improvised gadgets in the apartment. Inside his shower stall, the steamy inner sanctum of the recently deceased, I move aside his moldy stool and look around for signs of him, wondering whether the ghost hovering near the ceiling is calling louder to my mother than Ben's hands.

Despite the steam and the vodka, despite my earnest striving for anesthesia, I can't shut down the conveyor belt in my mind—can't stop the procession of twin coffins from advancing toward a deep dirt pit for two. Camus's opening line plays in my head: *Aujourd'hui, maman est morte*. Mother died today.

My mother is alive, technically—but she's a particle whose speed and direction are both currently unknown, her recent twitching notwithstanding. I recognize this moment as the big pothole in the avenue of our lives, and I have a feeling that all our tires will be flat before we get to the end of it.

Ten minutes later, when a timer goes off, I step out of the steam bath and flip off the wall switch, which sends enough juice up my arm to light up my teeth. I get a small dose of what my mother got under the rain hat and Margot's father got in his bath. Did someone perhaps forget to ground a wire?

Cured of jet lag, I cover the switch in Band-Aids and head to the kitchen for a checkup.

There, everyone is preoccupied. Ben is running the garbage disposal, which has just regurgitated a screwdriver and a week's worth of coffee grounds. Helen, meanwhile, is combing through the pantry, scraping together a meal from the "staples" that are supposed to save our lives in a disaster—Carnation condensed milk, a case of canned fruit in an emulsion that would give hummingbirds diabetes, and fifty packages of Jell-O, cherry-flavored no less. To distract my siblings from the appalling offerings, I recount the saga of my steam bath, but in the middle of my chronicle, the toaster bursts into flames. Helen puts the fire out with a wet dish towel, after which Ben sends me back to the bathroom for gauze to wrap her burn. My own case gets overlooked in the triage.

It's hard to avoid noticing that the kitchen—like the steam bath, the Cadillac, and, *oh, yes*, the boat—is an oversized booby trap. And everything is rigged to go off this holiday weekend.

Happy Memorial Day.

Our father, Mr. Fix It, dressed for home improvement in a worn gray jumpsuit, like the Maytag repairman, schlepping his matching toolbox around the house and the neighborhood. He didn't specialize. Mechanical, electrical, combustible, whatever. He had a particular fondness for internal-combustion engines, in cars and boats. Fortunately, he never had a chain saw.

He exalted puttering, and whether you asked him or not, he would happily tell you that his greatest joy in life was leaving things just a little better than he'd found them, in doing things "just so." Anyway, that was the concept. If he got wind that a neighbor's toilet was leaking or a shower needed grouting, he would dispatch himself to the scene, amiably rescuing friends who didn't want his help, pushing aside their qualms, their warranties, and their upcoming service calls to "take a little peek." Once he got in, there was no stopping him. Installing a showerhead—*woops*—he cut through Italian marble in the wrong place before finding just the perfect spot. And maybe he chipped the glaze off the bathtub, too. "So what? Who's gonna see it? And think of what it would cost to get that plumber, the highway robber, to make a house call on a Sunday."

Mort never understood why everyone was so ungrateful.

Up at the Shell station on Hope Street, where I often accompanied him, he was the garage groupie, hanging out with his aging jalopies, recombining them, eliminating parts that weren't absolutely necessary (like the catalytic converter), working away with his bulging purple tongue throbbing between his teeth—an image the school shrink had a field day with. When he worked in our driveway, Helen was the magician's assistant, turning on the ignition while he jumped the battery, standing downwind from the ether he doused on the carburetor, moving the door back and forth while he sprayed oil on the hinges. Helen and I knew we weren't Mort's first choice, that he would have preferred his son by his side in the driveway. But our "little Mozart" was inside practicing piano or listening to opera on the Victrola in his room.

The day my parents drove me to Connecticut College, where I got to reinvent myself, Mort tied my mattress to the roof of his old Ford station wagon. There was no reason for me to take a mattress to school, except that Mort knew I was on Valium, and since no one in our little nuclear family had anything really wrong in their heads, he attributed the prescription to a bad back. He strapped the mattress to the car roof, even though it was obvious that the smallest gust of wind would turn it into a hang glider. Lola ignored it, pretending to shuffle things—her bag, a hat, the radio. But I warned him. I could never resist predicting his disasters, and it didn't take Jeanne Dixon to see this one coming.

"Get in the car," he said, ignoring my advice. "I was tying knots before you were born." His tongue lopped out of the corner of his mouth like a chewed stogie.

Three miles south of Providence, as soon as the car hit fifty on I-95, not far from where he's about to be buried, the mattress began to plane and then took flight. He slammed on the brakes as gravel ricocheted like shrapnel off his perfectly simonized car until he brought it to a stop in the breakdown lane—which was increasingly a second home for our family, our memories there as indelible as skid marks.

When he opened his door, I felt the sucking vacuum of a passing truck. But despite the honking and the smell of burned rubber, I followed him out so I could look over his shoulder and taunt him. It's possible I was smirking.

"You should use a square knot this time," I said, honing my talent for noisy insubordination.

"It's not a scarf," he retorted, playing the gender card.

An hour later, Mort and Lola deposited me in a limestone castle on a glorious campus to study liberal arts, in the company of fourteen hundred women yearning for enlightenment and living by an honor code. Then it was roommate-bonding time, and the talk turned to *Beowulf* and matching bedspreads, and anyone who could play a guitar started strumming, while the rest of us prepared to hum along for four years.

Mort was already jangling his car keys when Lola made a futile effort to kiss me good-bye.

"You know," he said within earshot of my new roommate, "you're not as smart as you think you are."

This observation, Mort knew from practice, was a pin to the heart of my voodoo doll. According to him, my reach would always exceed my grasp. How could anyone ever *win* with that? How could I even get traction? While no one in our family was as smart as Lola, that was a shortfall we could accept: It was something we had in common. My father was so far beneath her that he competed only on the dance floor, and we three children knew our brains had been diluted before birth by his average strain.

In seventh grade, my friend Judy and I stole our homeroom teacher's notebook over a weekend. The theft was a breeze because the teacher was Judy's mother, and we broke into her desk at home while she was in church. We scoured that spiral notebook for grades and test scores, for personality inventories and psychological profiles, and on the last page, in the final column all the way to the right—a column I assumed was for IQ—I saw my official score, the most important number in the universe. My actual potential.

But—*oh nooooo!*—the score was crushing, and it was inescapable proof that I wasn't as smart as I thought I was. All summer, I carried the shame of that low number around with me, evidence of my intellectual weightlessness, bracing for failure when I started eighth grade in the fall. Surely with a number that low, junior high would be about as far as I could go. I reduced my expectations and narrowed my horizons, gave up on the idea of becoming a doctor, and wondered whether I was smart enough to become an orderly. Were Jewish girls ever orderlies?

And then, in the fall, the dreaded number turned out to be my new homeroom. I was relieved for a day, until I realized the number might also be my IQ. How could I ever know? Who could reassure me?

Lola believed I could do anything, despite what Mort said. I got tap lessons after I failed ballet, singing lessons after I failed piano—but I was good at none of it. Ben was "the musical one." The only place I did well was at school, and while I got good grades in grammar school, performance to date, as everyone knows, is never a guarantee of future returns. How soon would I exhaust my limited potential and reveal my inner utter averageness? The only solution was to study vigilantly, meticulously, obsessively, to make the most of whatever raw material I had. Late into the night, long after I'd finished my homework, I practiced Mensa drills under the covers with a flashlight, determined to take the exam if I ever felt sufficiently prepared. (I never did.)

So Mort's assessment was why I signed up freshman year in college for botany instead of chemistry, French instead of Chinese, and art instead of art history. I planned to avoid philosophy altogether and take religion to satisfy the college's "spiritual requirement," since everyone knew religion was easier. But Suzanne Forman, a junior in my dorm—and my nemesis—exposed me at breakfast, announcing to a packed room that I was afraid to take philosophy because I thought it was too hard for me. Suzanne, of course, *was* as smart as she thought she was and had aced philosophy. She shamed me into it.

Then the unthinkable happened: I turned out to be good at philosophy—at asking questions that have no answers, at teasing the metaphysical out of the mundane, at sorting through logical quandaries in a mostly losing quest for meaning and order. Who am I and why was I put here? What is real and what is mere appearance? What do I *really* know and how can I be sure

I know it? When people debate these kinds of questions, unless they're studying philosophy, they're generally institutionalized. It was the perfect major for the daughter of the center of the universe.

I was intoxicated by "the attempt to make sense of the whole of things" after a childhood where nothing added up. The more I studied, the more intriguingly perplexed I became. And I uncovered a natural talent for specious argumentation, which was mistaken for intellectual authority.

"But what are you gonna *do* with philosophy?" Mort kept asking, year after year.

Despite all the important questions philosophy examined, I had no idea what to do with it, so I just kept doing more of it. An insane amount of time elapsed, and I was on my way to a doctorate at a university near Boston.

My boyfriend at the time was a grad student whose field was the distinction between consciousness and thought. When I met him, I was so ignorant that I thought they were the same thing. Then I read his dissertation.

Am I conscious of my thoughts? Of course I am! Voilà, two distinct things.

My own dissertation, three hundred ponderous pages, was an insufferable, widely unread tome on skepticism, which proved logically that nothing can really be known, including the claim that nothing can really be known. A pointless argument to be sure, but a skillfully reasoned one that results in a squeamish paradox—where the truth makes you feel like somebody pulled a fast one. Philosophy felt like home to me.

But the search for the truth is a slippery slope. The minute that *philosophical discourse* begins, words get loaded and heavier—capitalized and hyphenated—and before you know it, the questions are piled higher and deeper than the answers, and you discover you know a lot less than you thought you did when you started out. "What is the truth" is not a new question, and so far, about 2,500 years into asking it, no one has provided a satisfactory answer.

Is there a reason for everything? Is there no reason for anything? Does it matter? Which is worse? How would you know?

In my fourth year of graduate school, at twenty-five, eight years into my metaphysical apprenticeship, I was asked to take over the Friday afternoon class of Philosophy 101. My first lecture was on the fundamental questions that confounded the ancient Greeks, who rhapsodized about the ineffable until dawn, especially when the moon was full and the wine was good. I had fifty sober minutes.

And yet—what to wear? I was so confused about how I should dress for the part—the first female teaching assistant in the department and only a few years older than the kids in the class. Should I dress up for respect or down for identification? Look like a learned authority or a fun gal? Schoolmarm or hot chick? Unfortunately, I leaned in the wrong direction and, deeply misguided about fashion, I stood on the stage before a hundred students to lecture on "Appearance and Reality," wearing white patent-leather go-go boots and a short jean skirt. I looked as if I'd stayed out all night at a dance hall and stopped by a brothel on my way to class. What could the students have thought? Well, who cares? Plenty of them were stoned, and most of them were taking the course pass/fail. Besides, my message was that appearances don't matter.

"What is knowledge?" I intoned, a five-foot-one-inch Platonist in a miniskirt. "You can only *really know* a thing if the thing itself is eternal and unchangeable. Because if the thing that you *thought* you knew suddenly changed, you could hardly be said to have known it. Which means that *everything* that changes—which is to say EVERYTHING in the material world—is fundamentally unknowable."

I'd laid out the issues in a minute. I smiled.

But no one smiled back. Half a dozen people in the back of the hall were yawning, when they should have been taking copious notes. They should have been writing down every single word I said, starting with "good afternoon."

"So how can we ever *know* what the truth is? What should we be searching for, and how would we recognize it if we found it? We live in a world of appearances, some false, all fleeting. And often the things that *seem* to be are *not*. Yet we're constantly called upon to decide and to act—even though we have no way of knowing *what* or *who* is real or true. Maybe nothing is what it seems to be. But how can we *know*? Even if we're all in agreement about everything around us, the world we agree upon may be nothing more than a universal illusion."

"Shit," somebody yelled out from the peanut gallery. "How can we go on?" And I lost all of them.

The student course critique rated teachers on a one-to-five scale—how *informative* they were, how *practical*, and how *deep*. I got a five on *deep* but did poorly on *informative* and *practical*. A little philosophy is a very good thing, polls show, but a little goes a long way.

When I met people off campus, everyone asked what my philosophy was. I'd been at it a long time, but I still didn't have a philosophy I could call my own. Initially, this embarrassed me, but it turns out that anyone who begins a sentence by saying "My philosophy is . . ." doesn't have one, either.

Mort's oft-stated philosophy, for example, was "Live and let live." And look where that got him.

"What do you do?" a man asked me one evening at a party where martinis flowed like sangria.

"Epistemology," I replied, already self-conscious, hoping that would be the end of it.

He looked at me blankly and turned to his wife for more information. She grimaced and pointed to her crotch. "*Ouch!*" she whispered to him before walking away from me. "The worst part of having babies."

After I'd been at it almost long enough to become a brain surgeon, I was deemed an official epistemologist—a rare species in very limited supply, although the small supply dramatically exceeded the demand. My thesis adviser had assured me that my dissertation would make me "more marketable." Its title was "The Irrefutability of Skepticism." What market could he possibly have been thinking of?

It all came to a meaningless end over Christmas in 1975, while I was part of a group grading blue books for the department chairman, although I was barely one chapter ahead of his class. Another teaching assistant found the same odd phrase in four students' exam answers: "fantasy echo." One student after another cited "fantasy echo culture" and "fantasy echo literature," especially in "fantasy echo Vienna." We had no idea what the term meant. I'd never even heard it, but I was hardly a scholar, and so I assumed that one student in the class had spent more time in the library than I, not much of a feat, and that the other three had plagiarized. So someone investigated.

In the old days, research in a library required patiently poring through card catalogs—which was one of the many reasons I never went there—but despite a heroic effort to ascertain a citation for the term *fantasy echo*, it simply did not exist. Because "fantasy echo" is what even the smartest kid in the class heard each time the professor said "fin de siècle." No one had understood a thing he'd said all semester. The problem of *other minds*, in a nutshell.

Belatedly, it dawned on me that I still had no idea what to do with philosophy and needed a *real* job, and despite my pedigree in skepticism, I settled on advertising. "It's a business of ideas," someone promised me, and I fell for it. I fell for the notion of creative thinkers who valued pithiness, who placed a premium on economy of words, who got as close as one could get to Hemingway without having to sustain anything longer than a thirty-second script.

So I took the job. And what a *fantasy echo* that turned out to be.

When I moved to New York, Mort awarded me his pièce de résistance, a five-year-old Chevy Caprice he had personally "maintained." Christine, as I named her, got stuck nearly everywhere I went. She had a broken ignition switch, and so I was always asking strangers to "give me a little push" or "roll me," acts that turned Christine on but made me feel promiscuous. When no one was around, I called AAA, having memorized their phone numbers throughout the greater New York and New England areas. The car still got me where I needed to go, even if it didn't always get me back.

Then my Caprice got more capricious. Her accelerator developed a mind of its own and plummeted down for no reason, making her lurch forward uncontrollably. To stop her, I had to put my left foot on the brake while simultaneously getting my right foot under the accelerator to release it. I had actually become quite adept at this, yet I knew that cars should not behave this way, and that it was not a good thing.

Since Mort trusted no one to work on his eroding fleet, I took the car back to Providence over a weekend. "Now what have you done?" was his welcoming comment when I pulled it into the driveway. He was a bit of a finger pointer. Up we went to the Shell station, six blocks with me driving and Mort in the death seat, but Christine failed to perform in the alleged manner. Grumbling that nothing was wrong, but indulging me nonetheless, he allowed me to drive onto the hydraulic lift so he could "take a peek" underneath.

Ever in control, my father, who had just heard the story of this car's willful self-propulsion, placed himself in the crawl space between the lift and the garage wall, directing me. "Roll it up. Roll it up." The dutiful daughter did as ordered, gradually edging the car onto the platform, at which point Christine turned maniacal and plunged down her accelerator, and I came within six inches of pinning my father to the wall. Which had always been appealing on a metaphorical level but was not one of my real life goals.

"Now what have you done?"

Shortly thereafter, Chevy recalled the Caprice to replace the accelerator cable.

On the late news the night before Mort's funeral, the Wakefield Rescue Squad drags a body bag from a powerboat. A crystalline sky frames the marina's name, Folly's Landing, a gift from the god of double entendres. It takes four firemen to heave the big black rubber sack, an oversized Hefty garbage bag with a zipper, which the newscaster identifies as my father. The pouch is carried down a dock to a waiting ambulance, where an attendant gives the stiff rubber-coated feet (or head) a shove before slamming the rear door. Next up is an interview with the doctor who discovered the couple, one in rigor mortis, the other, "well, who knows, poor thing. Given a little oxygen at the scene and taken off in an ambulance." The boat's generator had been running through the night and into the following afternoon, he reports, with the hatches and portholes closed, which—the newscaster points out—is not exactly safety protocol for a boat wedged in its slip.

The camera pans to the instrument of death, the *Mr. Fix It,* floating behind yellow police tape. I used to call the boat "*The Vomitorium,*" since everyone in the family puked on it, preferably in the head, but, on a busy day, maybe over the side if no one was looking. It was the center of our family life. Mort got everyone drunk on whiskey sours, while Lola's baked bologna and jelly snacks worked like an emetic. Every Memorial Day and Fourth of July, we motored into Narragansett Bay in our teacup-size starter "yacht," bobbing up and down in real yachts' wakes like a rubber ducky in a bathtub.

Ben turns off the news and sits down at Lola's old upright. Ironic to the end, he plays a Chopin barcarole that sounds like a sailor's song, its rhythm swaying like a boat rolling in the waves. Although there was precious little harmony growing up in our house, it was filled with music. Ben practiced from the minute he got home from school until Mort called for quiet during *Father Knows Best.* Then Ben trudged downstairs to the old spinet in our cellar and played the selection for *my* piano lesson, badly, so Lola would think I was practicing. He made Chopin the sound track of my childhood, and the melancholy nocturnes and heartbreaking ballades that poured out of him poured right into me.

But tonight, his playing is muddy. He stops in the middle of a passage, gets down on his knees and pulls out a silver fork that had been wedged behind the pedal. Then, he lifts the lid, and, piece by piece, he recovers place settings for eight. Had it been a grand piano instead of an upright, he might have found a tea service. Concealment of every kind was one of Lola's great gifts, a talent each of us imitated but never equaled.

When he was six, Ben was caught stealing (repeatedly) from Hall's, our local drugstore, and our father, barely hiding a smile, patted him lovingly on the head and dubbed him "The Blond Bandit." Punishment for the offense was dinner in his room, where he played (stolen?) piano recordings on his phonograph. He began by stealing small things, pencils and erasers and Band-Aids, and then, emboldened by his success and the light punishment, he graduated to comic books and notebooks and a stapler and, finally, a Barbie wedding dress for Helen, to be worn by the Barbie doll he'd already stolen for her.

Unfortunately, the pharmacist had been tailing him for weeks, recording the booty on prescription pads, and before Ben got out the door, Mr. Hall grabbed his shoulder and shook him down. Whereupon Barbie's white gown, veil, and heels slipped out from under Ben's shirt and hit the floor. Mrs. Hall came running down the aisle and asked if he wanted them gift wrapped.

Before bedtime, Ben wants to ransack Mort's possessions, searching for anything at the intersection of money and mortality. Wills and testaments, financial records, insurance policies, and the oft-mentioned but ne'er-disclosed key to his safety-deposit box—to which Ben's attached great urgency, although I'm betting it's empty.

"If anything ever happens to us—" Lola often began.

"Stop it, will you, Lola," Mort would say, interrupting her.

"They've gotta know about the key!"

That's as far as she'd get before they'd begin arguing about her fatalism and his fecklessness, and the conversation would devolve into old issues, and after an hour, they'd end up in bed having make-up sex. So we never learned where they kept the key or what was inside the box, but we were regularly reminded there was one.

What could be hidden in that damn box anyway? Mort's souvenir business was on the verge of bankruptcy. The little brick house we used to live in had two mortgages before he downsized it for the current rental. There was a deep pile of unopened bills on his desk, and the dunners were still calling during dinner. The wolf was at the door, baying behind the angel of death.

But my siblings want to have a scavenger hunt.

We start in the bedroom, which is decorated like a hothouse. The curtains are lush, the wallpaper is florid, and the sheets are on the verge of germination. Mood lighting is provided by a pair of Mort's fondue lamps, "sculptures" he assembled from fondue pots he found at the dump, sprayed a virulent brass color, and electrified—artwork constructed by a man who, upon arriving in Rome in 1957 to sell a line of brass souvenirs, told his guide that the ruins were a shambles and ought to be torn down.

Framed family photographs cover every surface—Ben stealing tulips from Roger Williams Park, Ben and Helen locked in the gingerbread house at Story Land, three stupefied children in front of the old Chevy on the road to Camp High Peak. Lola is smiling in every shot, but the three of us are scowling, brows furrowed, looking like we're wondering what the hell is going to happen next. Our childhood was directed by Lola and filmed by Mort, who stood behind his Leica, making us squint into the sunshine, and although he rarely got into the shot, he stood close enough to cast a shadow.

Between the two fondue lamps on his dresser is Lola's own sculptural triumph, "the Money Tree," a bonsai-size construction of Scotch tape and rounded toothpicks—the dull-tipped kind you can't hurt yourself with—with rolled-up dollar bills dangling from its branches like diplomas. Conceived at Shady Tree Sanitarium, it was her answer to Mort's persistent question, "Where do you think money grows?"

My father had plenty of money, she used to say, and even when he was broke, he had more than she grew up with. And so

Mort was caught between the invoice from Shylock and the demands of a manic spender (splurge-o-philia). He bought everything on time, but now his time was up.

I'm wondering whether it's time to start picking those dollar bills off the Money Tree, when Helen turns it upside down, and beneath it, tucked into its papier-mâché roots, she finds the Key.

There's no bank address or box number attached to it, only a scrap of paper with Hebrew letters in an ancient code Lola called "Gamatria"—a mind twister she learned from her grandfather, the great rabbi. His specialty was Talmudic anagrams. Unfortunately, he took the rules with him to the Infinite State, and our only translator is in a coma.

My siblings, exhausted and temporarily deranged, hatch a plot to raid the bank vault in the morning, before the funeral, even though they're not exactly sure which branch. That information is currently available only in Hebrew. Their plan is to talk their way into the vault of the Industrial National Bank downtown, using arguments they fail to disclose; then Helen is going to distract the guard, also unclear how, while Ben tries the key in various boxes. Crazy stuff, but they're not kidding. I know better than to try to talk them out of it.

Meanwhile, the two of them rummage through all the closets and drawers we'd been forbidden to touch as children, and they discover Mort's jewelry box. As the eldest, I assume the Form of Dubious Morality, resisting the ambivalent thrill of the break-in while recording its spoils: a Masonic ring (a gold knuckle breaker with a diamond chip), a pair of brass cuff links with fake rhinestones, and a threadbare appliqué embroidered *Mr. Fix It*, which fell off Mort's jumpsuit long ago and is itself in need of repair.

I knew my father's business was beyond repair, but the notion that he had nearly magical abilities to fix everything else was a fundamental precept of our family myth, which persisted despite all the evidence. Wasn't he always fixing something? Voilà! There's the proof. Circular, perhaps, but still.

Sure, his cars were always breaking down, but I attributed that to their age and number. I believed he could get any spark plug to fire, any motor to turn over, any wire to conduct current. He could get anything to start, but it took me years to realize he couldn't keep much going. On this night, when I should be sanctifying his memory, my inner critic will not shut up, will not be jollied out of its judgment by vodka, steam, or good taste.

In retrospect, all of his seemingly unrelated mishaps look like a game of connect the dots, like a straight line to calamity. Mr. Fix It's résumé of wrecks, his long record of jerry-rigging everything, had always been inconsequential. The breakdowns were even amusing, in a twisted way. That was just Mort. That was how he did things. "Hey, he always makes an effort," his friend George used to say, focusing on the positive, while he was probably wishing Mort would make his effort at somebody else's house. His catalog of errors was legion—rigged fuse boxes, a flying mattress, our driveway of motionless jalopies, cracked tile in bathrooms across the neighborhood—but they were all meaningless malfunctions. Maybe Christine's homicidal acceleration at the Shell station was a warning, but her effect was still benign. Nobody got killed.

Raiding Mort's jewelry box satisfies no one, and we move on. Ben finds a note from Lola tucked into Mort's dresser drawer, dated a week earlier, just a few days before the accident. Reading it would be an inexcusable invasion of privacy, so of course it's irresistible. Six hands, three minds, one thought. We've granted ourselves an inalienable right to investigate anything that has ever transpired between our parents, and neither death nor coma can abridge it. Mort is no longer a person; he has become "the deceased." His possessions enjoy no protection; they are "his effects." Lola—intubated and unconscious—is in no position to object. I have already lost my sense of their reality, and although I continue to feel that my father is hovering near the ceiling, radiating disapproval, that has never stopped me before.

Dear Mort,

You know I can't wait
for our Friday-night date,
'Cause I'm sure that your boat
will at last be shipshape.
Here's to our rendezvous
on the yacht prepped by you.
You will get your reward
when the evening is through.

I love you,
Lola

Our little family larceny is brought to an end by Lola's romantic couplets, playful words that have grown unexpectedly heavy. She had many unusual traits in her prime, but telepathy had never been among them. Now, from a coma, she is channeling irony.

Mort's boat was hardly "shipshape," as she undoubtedly suspected, and their Friday-night date was consummated with a death certificate.

The second coffin picks up speed.

Ben stays up all night, playing the piano furiously—first Chopin, then Liszt, and, inevitably, interminably, Rachmaninoff—nothing tranquil like a nocturne, but big noisy scherzos and a bombastic sonata or two. It is the music of wailing.

Lying awake on the pullout couch, listening to him, trying

to use his music to drown out my thoughts the way I did growing up, I am unable to get my mind off Lola in her seminal role on the way to camp—her Miss Universe impersonation, intoxicated by her own star power and her very centrality—and I try to imagine that force stilled in a persistent vegetative state. If my long-lost boyfriend was right, if consciousness and thought are two distinct things, then even in a coma, unconscious, Lola might still be thinking, spinning, but muted, locked in.

As for me—give me consciousness, or give me death.

The sun comes up. It's a crystalline day. And except for Mort, who got his reward Friday night, when the evening was through, and who is scheduled to collect it graveside this morning at ten, the rest of the family has made it all the way to Memorial Day.

So far, even Lola.

FOUR

Still Life

A hairy man sprouting bushy black eyebrows between a beard and a yarmulke pushes me into a dark library, chanting Hebrew prayers I don't understand. In the distance I hear organ music. Pulling out what looks like a *bris* knife, he slices and dices a sheet of black crepe like a sushi chef, and the sound of the crepe being slashed—being torn asunder—is a real grabber, so I know this is not a dream. But it is a symbol, which Rabbi Sternberg is only too willing to spell out. "The frayed threads," he says, "will keep unraveling like the fabric of life." Of course he's talking about Mort, but he pauses just long enough for me to see Lola, hanging by a crepe thread from death's waiting list, three days after the accident. Ben says he doesn't have a crystal ball, but he's given me a yardstick: "The longer the coma, the worse it'll be." In the meantime, we're having a funeral.

He's brusque, this man of the cloth, grabbing my shoulder

and then my lapel, manhandling me while he attaches a shredded badge of death to my best black Mugler suit. The flared shoulders and cinched waist have an old-fashioned movie-star allure, but the design is tongue-in-cheek, outré—perfect at Taillevent, but all wrong for a funeral in Cranston. I'm to wear the ragged crepe badge for thirty days, and after that, I'll have the stab holes in the silk suit to remind me.

The rabbi leads us through a creaky corridor to the main synagogue, a huge marble room with a cathedral ceiling, a room that filled up only on High Holy Days when I was growing up. But today the gathering spills out the doors and onto the sidewalks. My father on his own would have been a so-so draw, but this crowd thought they were coming for a double bill. The organ winds down as we come in through a secret door under the pulpit and take seats in the front row. Mort's brothers, two handsome misty-eyed men who look like younger versions of him, are sitting behind us, and they lean forward to say, "What a tribute the crowd is." I can't understand why they're counting the turnout but ignoring the timing, and the cause. Their older brother had just turned fifty-eight.

In my dream last night, he was a gust of wind, whistling for his toolbox.

What do you need it for? I asked.

I fix things, the breeze said breezily.

But aren't you downwind now?

You know, the wind whipped up, *you're not as smart as you think you are*.

So I threw a tiny lighter into the air, the Finesse he invented in the fifties but could never sell, and the draft that was my father exploded like the *Hindenburg*.

Now what have you done? he wailed.

And then he evaporated.

"What did *that* mean?" I asked Helen at breakfast.

"It meant," she said, "that his death notwithstanding, you're still trying to blow Mort away. Give it up already."

Sunlight is streaming through stained-glass windows, casting red and violet stripes on his unadorned casket. This is the first time I've been near it, though not the first time I've felt his dead presence. The coffin was nailed shut before I got here, and I wasn't invited to have a last look. "You don't want to" was all Ben would say. The smooth pine box looks like it was just dropped off from the factory, like anybody could be inside, and I can't help wondering if Mort is actually in this one. Maybe a stranger was hiding on his boat, disguised as him, and was gassed in his stead in the night. It's not like I've seen any proof that he's in there—the Hefty bag on TV had an airtight seal, too. I have no idea what he looks like or who dressed him or what he's wearing, whether he's going down in his favorite brown suit or in his gray mechanic's uniform. But I imagine he died gritting his teeth, with his purple tongue squeezed out of the side of his mouth, the way it did whenever he was doing detail work. I wonder if the undertaker was able to shove it back in or if it will stick out forever. "Don't make that ugly face," Mort used to tell me. "You never know when it'll freeze."

Rabbi Sternberg's eulogy sums my father up with the Teflon coating that death instantly conveys. There are imaginative passages about his business acumen, followed by embellished tales of his mythical standing as a handyman. I am cringing, but there's not even a trace of irony. Mr. Fix It is portrayed as an ingratiating hero, his toolbox ever at the ready, no task too daunting for his pluck. It's a light myth, our family cult, our little white lie, and everyone goes along with it, since the road to Mort's repair work was paved with good intentions. He was an amiable jerry-rigger who did the best he could, and despite ample evidence to the contrary, everyone thought that the stakes were low.

So I will not stand up at his funeral and go to the pulpit and tell the truth. I've come to bury Mort, not to praise him. I won't talk about Christine nearly flattening him at the Shell station, the dead weather radio on the stormy journey from the Vineyard, the copper pennies in the fuse box, the mattress that turned into a projectile on the interstate, the power steering that gave out on a country road, the Monza he gave Ben that burst into flames on Angell Street, the equipment in his brass factory—Startling Inventions—that chopped two fingers off my grandfather's hand. I won't talk about any of it, but the scenes replay in my head like the portents of disaster they were. My uncles are behind me, bawling inconsolably, and they don't speak up, either. Only the rabbi is willing to go on record. And mostly, he lies.

Organ music swells as we rise to our feet. The words *sanctified* and *magnified* and *glorified* are repeated again and again, and I recognize this as the closer. Arms reach out to comfort me, and people I barely recognize push one another out of the way to grab my hand, as if I'm a rock star. Despite my fury, I've filled up my ration of Kleenex with a river of mucus. The crepe threads have been snipped of their weak links. *Après ça, le déluge*.

Twenty minutes later, our entourage gets off I-95 at the Jewish cemetery in Warwick. This spot at the edge of a clover-leaf, surrounded by bumper-to-bumper traffic and futile honking that could, well, wake up the dead—this will be my father's final resting place. A canopy has been set up over the headstones of his parents and aunts and uncles, and a fresh hole has been dug nearby for him. Next to my front-row seat is a second plot, reserved for Lola, where the ground is so soft that it must have been refilled while we were driving here. Mort is the first of his generation to arrive, a distinction he wasn't born to but has earned on his own, and already I hear his cousin Sid, who by rights should have been next, trying to lighten the moment by joking that Mort never could wait his turn.

The rabbi is giving a sermon now, explaining that the shredded crepe ribbons represent anguish and anger, which reassures me that I'm on track so far. The shoveling ceremony, which is up next, will usher in acceptance and reconciliation. That seems like a tall order, since I've barely begun to explore my bitterness. Nevertheless, we get to our feet, and Mort is lowered into the ground as we sing. The guttural chant, which I can't translate but know by heart—d'*chhhhub* d'*chhhhaw*, b'*hahachhh* b'*chaw*—mounts in my throat like a hair ball. This was the moment at my grandfather's funeral when my grandmother tried to throw herself into his grave. "I'm going with you, Monty," she screamed, like an Indian queen ready to sacrifice herself on her maharaja's pyre. She never lost her burlesque touch, and my brother had to restrain her that day. There'll be no such histrionics this time. My own generation lacks the talent, and our mother is otherwise engaged.

Being next of kin, I'm first in line for the spade, ready to cue the reconciliation theme. The rabbi instructs me to use the back of the shovel to symbolize regret, but before anyone can stop me, I turn the tool around and unleash a landslide. Sticks and stones are thundering against Mort's pristine casket, pummeling it, and I'm prepared to keep shoveling for as long as it takes—until the big wedges of my anger are beaten into small slices of acceptance. Only when a huge rock, a ten-pounder I carefully select and heave, hits the casket so hard that it cracks, only then does my brother grab the shovel from my hand and give me a horrified look. *What?* Am I the only one who read this morning's paper, where the photo of Mort in a Hefty garbage bag made page one, next to an article on proper powerboat safety?

Ben sprinkles pebbles on Mort and drops a toy screwdriver

into his grave as deaf Cousin Izzy comments loudly enough for all to hear, "I never trusted him. Jewish men aren't handy."

Why didn't Cousin Izzy bother to point that out earlier, say a week ago?

"He really screwed up this time," I whisper to Helen.

"We all screw up. Daddy got caught."

My sister, unlike me, is a forgiving person, and after she gently drops a thimble of sifted white sand into Mort's lonely pit, she casts the Mr. Fix It patch on top of him, lovingly.

In the "cemetery social hall," over cocktails, the rabbi explains that the meal of condolence calls for round foods like lentils and hard-boiled eggs, symbolizing the cycle of life. But to help us regain our strength, a bar has been set up at each end of the room, and long buffet tables are being filled with barbaric mounds of corned beef and pastrami to satisfy the acute need Jewish people have to stuff themselves with fat before sitting shiva.

Mort's friends tell tender, warm reminiscences about him and a few jokes about his botched house calls. I hear a crack about cracked bathroom tile, but no one dares bring up the boat. They all seem to be pretending that the stories of his life have nothing to do with his death. They marvel at how young he looked, as though youthfulness could still be a compliment for a man who's been buried before turning sixty and is now one huge splinter. I envision him in the dark, under the avalanche, smothered in pale gray polyester, with wood shards shoved under his fingernails.

But hardly anyone can finish a sentence about Lola. "We hope your mom . . ." is what I keep hearing, followed by a dubious but encouraging grimace, a sniffle, and a squeeze of my hand. No one has the vaguest idea what to hope for.

"What's the worst that could happen?" That's what Jewish people usually ask, as though whatever it is, if we just say it out loud, we can deal with it. We've dealt with worse before. "The worst that could happen" is supposed to provide perspective. But this time around, I can't figure out what it is. And no one, not one single person, dares to ask. *I* certainly don't, and my brother the doctor has been standing right here. "Answer the patient's questions" is his rule of thumb. "If they don't ask, they don't want to know." What safe questions can I ask about a woman who's barely squeezed out of a refilled grave and has been hooked up for seventy-two hours to a ventilator in a hospital at the beach where she lies in a "comma," waiting for final punctuation?

The center of the universe has stopped spinning and been sucked into a dark hole where there is nothing. Where even if there were something, she wouldn't know it. Where even if she knew it, she couldn't communicate it. That is how the ancient Greeks defined nonexistence. Maybe Ben was technically wrong about a double funeral, but Lola is hanging by a crepe thread that's still unraveling. *The longer the coma, the worse it'll be*. How good could it be? How good was it even before the accident?

Toward the end of a receiving line so long that my uncles are *qvelling* again, there's a handsome man in his late fifties, with a lot of dark wavy hair and a well-tailored suit. He's nodding at me in that respectful way strangers nod at the bereaved, and I'm nodding back at him because his teeth are so white. Wondering if he's too old for me. Would it be karma if I met a man at my father's funeral? Would it be creepy if the man was my father's age?

Harvey Diamond introduces himself as a golf buddy in Mort's foursome and hands me a business card engraved WRONGFUL DEATH LITIGATION.

"*Wrongful* death?" I ask.

"A death caused by negligence," Harvey says. "Like your dad's, I'd venture."

Haven't we just buried the defendant? my sneer must convey.

He raises an eyebrow, an expression I bet he's practiced in front of a mirror, as if he knows something the jury doesn't.

"Liability is relative," he whispers, leaning in until I can smell cream soda on his breath. "Juries never put *all* the blame on the victim."

Just then, Ben, who's been across the room on the phone, pacing in small circles and wringing his fingers through his thinning brown hair, hangs up and rushes toward me like he's caught fire. He pulls me away from Harvey and delivers the news I both long for and dread.

"The coma is lifting."

At last. The curtain is rising.

Ben leads Helen and me out the door and into the black limo and on to whatever is waiting. I can't remember a time when we were together in a backseat without our parents up front, telling us to be quiet or they'd separate us. Well, we're still together, but we're quiet now.

After a while, I tell them the dream I had on the plane, about the mysterious old woman in the hospital bed, and the blank newspaper that only the nun could read, and the clock without hands.

"What was the nun reading?" my red-eyed sister asks, leaning forward to make eye contact like the professional she is, even though she's unable to stop sniffling.

"She was reading a story, but I don't know what about." I shrug.

Helen presses me. "Another word for *story* is . . ."

"Feature, column, editorial." There's a prayer book in the back of the limo, but no thesaurus.

"Could the nun have been reading an article? An article of *faith?*"

My sister probably uses the Socratic method when she has more time, but it's a long dream and a short car ride, so she drops big hints. "Maybe she can see it because she's a believer. But you're a skeptic, so you can't."

My credentials as a skeptic are unassailable. "So what about the broken timepiece?"

"Well, you were stuck in an airplane, so of course time was standing still. That's pretty obvious. But you used two different words. You called it a 'timepiece' and a 'clock.' You never called it a *watch*."

I nod.

"And it had no hands, meaning *you* had no hands. You were helpless. It was a *death*watch and there was nothing you could do."

Helen smiles. She's proud of herself. I'm proud of her, too.

"Can you figure out who the old woman was?" she asks.

Ben pops open a prescription bottle and hands me a little yellow pill. *Veni, Vidi, Valium*.

Of course I know who the old woman was in the dream, but what I can't quite see is who she's going to be now. Here in Wakefield. Now that the deathwatch is over, what comes next?

Lola, unlike Sunny von Bülow, is scheduled to wake up. But not the way Sleeping Beauty woke up, in a fairy tale, dressed for success. With Lola, we have to "be prepared for brain damage," a phrase that unravels the remaining threads of my crepe ribbon. How exactly does one *prepare* for brain damage? What can I buy? How do I brainproof a house? I know dozens of synonyms for *insanity* in several languages, but *brain damage* is a big clump of a term I've never had to deconstruct. I don't know its hallmarks or its subtleties and I barely know how to define it. What is it that happens to the oxygen-deprived after they're given a little oxygen and rushed from the scene? What happens after the brain swells like a soufflé in a sealed pan? The recipe for life in general and the brain in particular is 70 percent water. My brother is worried that Lola's source has dried up, damming her flow, turning her neurological tributaries into parched land. I've overheard his whispered phone calls—his references to "cerebral sequelae"—and the term is both serious and mysterious, like a veil of gauze over a festering wound.

The longer the coma, the worse it'll be.

But what if Lola's brain *isn't* damaged? What if she stays the way she was? That's the big elephant in the backseat with us—the lunatic she is when she's "normal." How are we supposed to manage her without Mort, her wrangler, who, when the going got tough, when push came to shove came to butter knifing, could at least be counted on to take her on a road trip or get her an electrical sabbatical?

It's easy to envision the old woman in my dream leaping from her hospital bed when she comes to, screaming and thrashing like she's being exorcised. I've seen that. I've heard her first dry shrieks and then the thicker mucus of her hysteria. I've seen nurses try to jolly her back to bed "until the shot kicks in." Which one of us will stand watch during her restless, drug-induced sleep? Who will wrestle her back to bed for the second shot? When will the normal sludge of her mourning descend into the bedrock of madness? And who will oversee the Herculean struggle to commit her to Shady Tree?

Now that Mr. Fix It has gone underground, who's in charge?

Our Lady by the Sea is miles from the ocean, floating on hot asphalt, with a Hail Mary entrance hall confirming my otherness. But Ben knows the way—left at the life-size Madonna, right at the baby Jesus, straight through the heavy swinging pearly-colored doors, where it's warmer, quieter, and emptier, until we reach the end of a pale green corridor and enter a room full of monitors. There, floating under a crucifix in diffuse white light, lies a small, faintly pink, very still woman hooked up to equipment I can't identify. Aerated and irrigated and tethered to monitors like a science experiment. This network of wires and tubing is my mother.

Ben is already at her side, tracking us through the machinery like a pilot sweet-talking passengers through a crash landing. He explains in a hypersoothing tone how the dead-looking woman pulled out her breathing tube this morning while we were burying Mort, so now she's underneath the kind of plastic that once covered our living room furniture.

Lola's features are hidden, mysterious. Vapor rises from her face and condenses on the tent, framing her in fog like the Delphi oracle. But the apparatus limits her pronouncements, which are all I am waiting for, and dreading.

I've come to her bedside expecting the worst, based on precedent, or whatever could count as precedent in this singular situation. What is unknowable about Lola, though, is the exact shape one's worst expectations will take—exactly what she'll do and how long it will take her to do it. Especially without Mort. She's a contradictory jumble of power and fragility, for whom "too much pressure" was Mort's code, and a new dose of pressure is about to test her threshold.

I'm the last to approach, as usual, hanging in the doorway like the phobic candy striper I was twenty years ago—and in my dream last night—resigned to touching some part of her, but preferably a part that's unwired. I settle on her feet. And now that I'm up close, I can see her face is blank, not at all what I expected. Her big brown doe eyes stare into the mist, empty, unreadable, unblinking. There's no chance she's bolting from the bed anytime soon.

Ben plants himself squarely in front of her and pushes his nose up against the tent.

After a while, her eyes crawl to his.

Then her mouth opens a little and vapor escapes.

But there are no words.

"Mom? Mom?" he shouts, sounding like an air-raid siren.

Helen starts hollering, too. "Mom? Can you hear me? Can you hear me?" It's as though Lola's disappeared and they've joined a search party.

I am standing by.

Despite all this attention, Lola appears unmoved. The mist whooshes around her tent, clouds behind a scrim, and some lyrics I never understood from a song I never liked start playing in my head.

It's cloud's illusions I recall
I really don't know clouds at all

That's when I always changed the station, so I have no idea what words come next. The "cloud" couplet is stuck on repeat. Minutes pass, a half hour, maybe more . . . *It's cloud's illusions I recall* . . . and though her eyes are open, she's unresponsive as a mummy.

Ben and Helen take turns trying to rouse her, dueling foghorns, while I stand by the window like a dunce, hiding, squeezing my eyes shut, hyperventilating, listening to them yell, "WAKE UP, MOM, WAKE UP," while I am mute and useless. It takes all my energy just to keep up my guard, since the real Lola could be lurking inside the still body and could spring out without warning. Any minute the sound track could switch from Judy Collins to *Jaws*.

But that doesn't happen.

What happens is that Lola's shaky pink hand finally rises an inch and moves slowly toward her eyes.

She blinks.

She examines her fingers.

Her lips tremble.

They begin to move.

She's going to speak.

And we all lean forward into the orbit of the center of the universe, a whirlwind no more, waiting for her first fearsome words.

"Where's my jewelry?" Lola asks. Her voice is as wobbly as a worn-down phonograph, but she holds up both hands for all to see.

Even Ben is speechless.

With her cardiac monitor beeping like a metronome, my brain tries to piece together the information that makes sense: a confused woman in a hospital bed under an oxygen tent, eerie fluorescent backlighting, three children circling, dressed in black. Given these pictures in a Mensa test, I could organize a coherent narrative. They fit. But the audio track is coming from a different story. Lola's words hang in the air, while what's unsaid—the missing script that begins "Mort is dead!"—is bursting in me. Shouldn't someone yell "Cut!" and call for the right lines? Where is her bloodcurdling scream? Her leap from the bed like Tosca jumping to her death? The chase down the hallway? The orderlies screaming "Calm down, calm down," surrounding her, pinning her down, shooting her up?

But while I'm waiting like a catatonic for someone else to take charge, I notice her fingers do lack their usual sparkle. The big solitaire Helen dubbed "the Headlight" and the baguette pileup known as "the Train Wreck" are nowhere to be seen. How often we'd all been chastened about their sentimental value and had promised never, no matter what, to sell them. Now both rings are missing, and although I had nothing to do with their disappearance, I feel as guilty as if I'd stopped by a pawnbroker on the way to the ICU.

"What happened to my nail polish?" the shaky voice asks next.

She holds up four red nails and a colorless thumb, jamming my mind in a childhood rhyme. *He put in his thumb and pulled out a plum.* Then what? What comes after the plum?

The whereabouts of Lola's jewelry is unknown, Ben explains, but her nail polish was removed by a paramedic to see if there was any oxygen left in her tissue. After she'd been dragged from the boat. As she lay unconscious on a dock. With nary a manicurist in sight.

The précis seems to satisfy her.

"You came all the way from Paris," she says gratefully, as though I could have phoned in my regrets if I'd had other plans. As though it's very generous of me to make such an effort on her behalf.

Do I say "you're welcome; it was nothing," or should I fess up and say "I came for Mort's funeral"?

I say nothing.

"You got here fast," she says, picking up the slack.

I smile. I squeeze her foot. I'm not prepared for small talk about the speed of aerial transport, even though it's a safer topic than the speed of death.

Could someone please get to the point?

"You've been in the hospital for three days, Mom," Ben begins.

Hold on, here we go.

"It's okay. I'll be out soon."

Like this is just a hiccup.

"We need to talk to you about Daddy," Helen says, sweet-talking her, reaching under the tent, and taking Lola's hand. Ben goes around the other side and takes her other hand. Maybe they rehearsed this, or maybe they just have an instinct for it.

I keep one eye on the door, ready to chase her if she tries to make a run for it. Or to make a run for it myself if things get really out of hand.

"The nurses told me," Lola says, waving her hand dismissively, like Mort is old news.

"You *know* about *Daddy*?" Helen asks, her eyes bulging like Joan Crawford's.

"Yes, it's okay."

It's "okay"? Here we are, at the moment I've been dreading, and the woman in the hospital bed is unruffled. Where is the screaming banshee who raised me? This woman is unrecognizable, so tranquil, so *understated—too* understated.

She turns to Ben. "You did everything you could to save him."

"*Me?*" Ben asks. "What could *I* do? Daddy died on the boat in the middle of the night, before I got there."

"Yes," she replies.

"Too bad," she adds a beat later, shaking her head from side to side, as though we're commiserating about someone she played gin rummy with a couple of times in the fifties but hasn't thought about since.

"Is the boat okay?"

Hello? Mort is dead! The boat is in dry dock. It's roped off by yellow police tape, illuminated by floodlight, and reeking of vomit. Every step has been taken to keep it from starting up again. Its key is in a sealed envelope in a locked safe in a police precinct. The police toxicologist is planning to test the generator's output after donning a gas mask in a monitored environment, with an ambulance standing by. To plot the precise parts per milliliter of carbon monoxide it delivers over time. As though the evidence isn't already six feet under—and right here before us.

"The boat's fine," Helen tells her, lying.

Lying is good. Lying reminds me of happier times.

"Do you remember anything?" Ben asks.

His question surprises me, since the neurologist already told him Lola wouldn't recall the ordeal. "The traumatized brain is unable to form memory," the expert intoned. There followed a long discourse between them on the chemistry of messenger RNA, a discussion I was spared. But this learned conclusion was based on the average brain, and Lola's brain is hardly average.

Her photographic memory announced itself when she was barely out of diapers, when she beat her father and two of his cronies at Concentration. They weren't the brightest lights and they might have had a few, but to be beaten by a two-year-old said something about the child. In college, she was accused—falsely, it turned out—of cheating on a surprise quiz on the periodic table after she replicated all the elements from hydrogen to argon, along with their symbols and atomic weights, while the rest of the class flunked. Everyone said she had the brains of her grandfather, the illustrious Rabbi Bachrach. A mixed blessing, to be sure. So despite the expert neurological nay-saying, Ben asks what she remembers.

"We put the boat in the water. We went out to eat. We had scotch and steaks."

Her voice is halting, but her facts are clear: what they did, where they did it, and, of course, the menu.

Ben and Helen exchange smiles, proud of her in some insane way that goes beyond her simple recitation. The fact that Lola can remember *anything* defies medical expectation. Either her messenger RNA is Olympic or she's making it up.

But now that she's speaking in paragraphs, I realize there's something eerie about Lola's delivery. It's a pinched, robotic monotone. There's no change in her pitch or tempo, and her words are staccato.

"It. Was. Cold. I. Told. Mort. Turn. On. The. Heat."

A ghostly cloud drifts past her face while she pauses. Although she's been expressionless until now, something like a smile spreads over her face.

"We made love."

Why is she already talking about sex? Couldn't she limit the details to their last supper? Where the hell is her internal censor?

"It was very good," she adds.

She may be in an oxygen tent in an ICU after three days in a coma, but character will tell: Here lies the hypersexual Lola, who showed up at my French-themed going-away party in a black miniskirt and red patent-leather fuck-me pumps, announcing (unnecessarily) that she'd come as a prostitute from Pigalle. After a trip to the bathroom, she returned with her miniskirt draped over her shoulders, tucking her low-cut blouse into her fishnet panty hose. My father, in a black beret and an oily false mustache, came as her pimp.

In the sixties, at their backyard "limbo parties," Mort was bartender, topping off everyone's whiskey sours while Lola turned up the stripper music and lit the tiki lamps. Three or four couples from the neighborhood lined up on the lawn, taking turns doing an odd spastic thing under a bamboo stick, insisting it was dancing, throwing their shoulders back and their knees into the air and twitching their legs like grasshoppers. Even then I sensed the contest was really about the twitching, since no one seemed to give a shit when they knocked the stick down, and no one was ever disqualified. Lola was especially good at it. When she was in the final throes of her air-thumping, it looked like she wasn't wearing underpants.

"Do you remember anything else, Mom?" Ben asks, changing the subject.

"Daddy was red. Like he was blushing."

"It was the carbon monoxide," Helen whispers. She's trying so hard to control herself, she's gagging. Helen was the one who hung out in the driveway with Mr. Fix It while Ben, his favorite, stayed in the house, practicing piano, and I hid under the covers with an endless parade of transitional objects. "We had to bury Daddy this morning. The rabbi wouldn't let us wait."

"I know. It's okay."

"It's a miracle you're alive," Helen says, gazing up at the painting of the Virgin Mary above Lola's bed. She starts to cross herself before realizing Lola doesn't know she just converted to Catholicism to marry her Irish boyfriend.

"That's nice," Lola says.

Mort must be rolling over.

Then this strangely composed person in our mother's body lies back calmly in her plastic tent on her cloud of hyperallergenic pillows and motions toward the door, signaling us to leave.

"I'll be home soon. I'll be fine. Don't worry."

And off she drifts to sleep.

Once we're in the hospital cafeteria, the analysis begins. It's hard to put my finger on what's missing from Lola, since the presence of something is so much easier to describe than its absence. But her serenity makes her unrecognizable, as though someone pressed the mute button on her personality. Self-pity would be appropriate. Hysteria was predicted. But there's no grief. She's lock-jawed in her self-restraint, even without benefit of a straitjacket. Whither the sudden perspective? And *what* is wrong with her voice?

"She pulled the breathing tube out of her own throat," Ben reminds me.

That's gotta hurt. But still, why does she talk like a robot?

"The poisoning was like being hit over the head with a frying pan about a thousand times," Ben says, and I see Olive Oyl beating herself with a cast-iron skillet, exclamation points flying out of her noggin. "Her brain swelled inside her skull, and believe me, there's not a lot of extra room there. Then the boat stewed her in the sun for half a day, when the medical protocol calls for ice. Can you imagine what she lived through? It's amazing she didn't stroke out. I can't figure out what kept her alive, when Mort was already in rigor mortis."

Ben is full of consoling images, like this one of our father as a stiff plank.

My brother the doctor and my sister the psychologist trade jargon like a pair of brainiac monitors, congratulating each other as though Lola has won the lottery. And in a way, I suppose she has. Ben calls her night on the boat "the stress test of all time" and predicts she'll live to be a hundred. Helen nicknames her "Big Heart." So even before we leave the cafeteria and return to her bedside, two of Lola's mildly manic offspring are already on the upswing.

I wish I could catch what they have, but I can't shake the feeling that my mother is dead. That the robot in her bed is a pod without its pea. Ashamed as I am of my Valium-enabled detachment, I'm sane enough to keep it to myself. Instead of talking, I start nodding, pretending to go along with their conspiracy of optimism.

"It hasn't hit her yet," they say. "She's in shock."

"Shock" makes sense to me, and since they're the professionals, I subscribe to their diagnosis. Although I have no idea what *shock* is. Whether it's metaphor or fact. Whether it's physiological or psychological, or both. Whether it lifts on its own or has to be exorcised. And by the time they're deep in discussion, it's too late for me to ask for a definition, because I've been nodding for ten minutes, pretending to understand.

No doubt they're wielding *shock* precisely, like a scalpel, but for me it's a blunt linguistic grab bag.

No tears? *Shock.*

Robotic tone? *Shock.*

Cotton-headed priorities? *Shock.*

Pornographic description of her evening activities? *Definitely shock.*

Well, maybe the sex spiel is normal for her, but it's still shocking to me, even after all these years, and especially at this moment. Copulating on the threshold of Mort's death seems like necromancy. It turns me into a voyeur again, the little girl at their door, listening despite myself.

Don't make her lick it all.

Not a terrible way to go, really.

When his heart exploded, it was so good, she thought he was blushing.

FIVE

Origin of the Species

The day that Mort is laid to rest, Lola is taken off the danger list and upgraded from intensive care to a private room. I'm betting there's no connection between his being grounded for good and her rising from metaphorical ashes, but both of my siblings are looking vaguely otherworldish. No one says it out loud, but I have a feeling Ben has that whole *K2* thing going on in his head, wondering whether it was his fingers on Lola's temples that made her finally let go of Mort.

My own view is that a six-foot-deep dirt avalanche is a hell of a dark tunnel for a bright white light to shine through. But I'm grateful that Ben threw a toy screwdriver into Mort's grave instead of a shovel.

Now that the carbon-monoxide glow has faded from her skin, Lola's as blanched as the rest of us. She's plumped up on pillows and out from under the tent, with just an oxygen mask draped around her chin, the mist rising from her face like steam, as though she's having a facial.

Ben is cheerful, handsome, glowing with pulmonary pride. Today I would cast him as Dr. Kildare.

Helen catches his mood spontaneously, while I try to fake it.

Plastic tubes ferry pale yellow liquid from under Lola's sheet to a steel repository below her bed, while clear fluids drip in through her arm—persistent signs of forced irrigation. She's conscious, though, which is the good news, although it could also turn out to be the bad news. The medical team has pronounced her "stable," but they're measuring only her vital signs. I have additional criteria.

This is the moment when I expect to see her brave demeanor crumble and the floodgates open, when she could bolt from the bed and make a run for it.

Shouldn't somebody be readying a syringe?

The wan atmosphere, though not the anxiety, is relieved by Ben, who's brought along the treasures from our scavenger hunt in Mort and Lola's bedroom. Like pulling a rabbit out of a hat, he reveals the key to the safety-deposit box, which is still taped to her Hebrew anagram, and he's craving instruction that will point us toward a vault stuffed with stock certificates, loose diamonds, and a credit card that isn't maxed out.

Lola pushes her mask aside and a moist cloud lifts off. She takes the key from Ben's hand and examines it. Then she tucks it under her sheet. "I'm alive, aren't I?"

End of discussion.

And she has a point, but it's hard to ignore the context.

Moving on—because she has her own agenda—she hands Ben a scrap of paper with scribbling on it. "Mail this."

In my dream the night before, the old woman in a hospital bed handed me a slip of paper, and when I tried to read it, it was blank. What could *this* woman in a hospital bed, fresh out of a coma, have written? A final will and testament? A farewell note to her three beloved children? An account of her near-death experience?

Over Ben's shoulder, I decipher her shaky handwriting.

Dear Nantucket Dockmaster,

We can't come in July
And here's the reason why.
My Captain has just died.

Sincerely,
Mrs. Hornstein
PS: Please return my twenty-five-dollar deposit.

"Shock," Helen whispers.

"Shock," Ben concurs.

"Shock," I repeat.

Undeterred, Ben moves on to the ring, Mort's Masonic ring, a gold testosterone tribute with a diamond flake. It's our second clue and a profound symbol of . . . of *what*, exactly? I have no idea whatsoever.

Aside from the Mr. Fix It patch (which Helen has just thrown into his grave), Mort left very little of himself in his jewelry box—a pair of brass cuff links with matching tie clip (for which no one has any affection) and this ring, which Ben's been carrying around in his pocket and rubbing like a totem. It's not much jewelry for a man who, like almost everyone else in Providence, was once in the jewelry business, and it wouldn't be much fodder for imagination—except that none of us knew he was a Mason. Discovering this secret—his allegiance to a sect other than the mechanics' union—makes Mort enigmatic in death, lending him a note of complexity, like a young wine with a big bouquet.

Slipping the ring onto his finger, Ben displays his bejeweled hand to Lola like a peacock—proud and expectant, yearning.

Her face sags. "*Don't wear the ring.*" Her tone is cryptic, disquieting, and full of unmistakable doom.

"But wasn't it *Daddy's?*" Ben's hell-bent on finding meaning, and Lola, awakened from her magic sleep, needs to provide it.

"DON'T WEAR *THE RING*," she repeats, louder now, like it's cursed.

She's channeling Erda the Earth-Mother, who warned the king of the gods to return the ring he stole or be damned.

I'm inclined to take Lola's word for it, given whose ring this was, and I'd be happy to chuck it into the hazardous-waste bin. Maybe she thinks it's disrespectful to wear a dead man's jewelry. Maybe there's more to Mort's Masonic history than we need to know. Or maybe she thinks the ring has transformative powers.

When Lola was in her thirties, not so long ago, she insisted that certain people in the family had been replaced by impostors who were plotting against her. Voices were calling her name, warning her. "Obsessional rumination," her shrink said at the time. "Paranoid delusions."

Lola's explanation was pithier: "Aunt Flossie is taking over my thinking again."

Aunt Flossie, my grandmother's youngest sister, lived in Flushing, where she was preoccupied with her quiet life of alternate-side-of-the-street parking—so her takeover of Lola's brain was long-distance. But I knew from an early age that Flossie references were not to be taken lightly, that "Aunt Flossie" was a sign things were about to go from pretty bad to much worse. "Aunt Flossie" meant the curtains would be drawn, even in sunlight, and there would be house calls. It meant "the elders" would assemble in the living room, begging Lola to "forget about it," although "it" hadn't yet been clarified for me. Lola wanted "the truth about what happened," but the elders were not in favor of that. Which was not a new position for them, from what I'd heard over the years.

Once Aunt Flossie took over her thinking, Lola came undone in our living room in a star turn with Greek chorus. "The children, the children," my grandmother would cry, pointing to me hiding behind a chair, trying to follow the clues that were inadvertently dropped and quickly swept up. But despite their subterfuge, around the time I was nine, I deduced that Aunt Flossie, who everyone knew was an irredeemable nutcase, was not Lola's aunt after all. Aunt Flossie was her biological *mother*. The woman in the room whom Lola called her mother—my savior—was actually her aunt, Flossie's sister.

Certainly *some* people were changing identities—and you didn't have to be crazy to feel confused.

Not to say my mother wasn't crazy. She was. And the explanation involved both of the usual suspects: heredity and environment. Aunt Flossie ran in her genes, and what Bill made her do unraveled the twisted strands of her DNA.

Here is where it began. In the maternity ward on the day after Lola's birth, Flossie, tipping over the edge of postpartum depression, like her sisters before her, snarled that the redheaded baby cradled in her redheaded husband's arms wasn't his.

So long Red.

Hello psych ward.

Flossie had eight siblings who might have raised her baby, but the choices narrowed if sanity was a strict criterion. The eldest sister was in and out and in again, and no one dared ask the two brothers—with their legal problems. Flossie's father, the rabbi, decided that the best option was Leah—his youngest, childless daughter, a twenty-seven-year-old tap dancer in a family of Brown-educated intellectuals. Her "million-dollar legs" had recently retired from George White's *Scandals* on Broadway and were currently appearing behind the counter at a deli on North Main Street in Providence. She was a saucy cardsharp and sometime bookie, with a laugh like sugar candy and a shimmering heart of gold. While she might have been the nutty relative on anyone else's family tree, in our family she was a paradigm of mental stability. She saved Lola, and she saved me, too.

Leah named the baby after a rich cousin from Philadelphia, Leibalah, figuring there were good odds a fat check would follow. Leibalah lasted until the check cleared, and after that, everyone called the baby Lola.

"Nana saved us," I told my mother when she got home from one of her trips to Shady Tree in the fifties.

"She's trying to turn you kids into criminals," Lola said, correcting me. "And thank God I'm back to rescue you."

"Bingo is going to make us criminals?" I laughed, sloughing it off.

"Bingo and poker and the track and the pool hall. And *the stories*."

"She's just trying to cheer us up."

"So why doesn't she take you to the park or the skating rink?"

This, of course, was a question of taste. Nana knew how to have a good time.

"We got caught" was the opener of Nana's best bedtime story. It was more of a brag than a confession, because her moral fiber was fuzzy and she was proud of being a bad girl. She made getting caught sound naughty but nice. The details involved "drivin' a truck across state lines," and whatever else "state lines" were, they made her big brown eyes get bigger. My grandmother was barely five feet tall. She had to stretch to see over the dashboard of my grandfather's Lark, and she didn't even have a driver's license. So it was impossible to envision her barreling down back roads alone in the dark in a big old truck with its lights turned off to avoid "the feds," with a Derringer in her purse and a dozen bottles of something called "hooch" in the wheel wells. But that's what she claimed. I thought she made the whole thing up. Like most things she told me as a child, my grandmother's account of getting caught was delivered long before I could comprehend it. She filled my head with characters I was too young to understand and words she didn't bother to define.

"You're a real back rack," she used to tell me when I was a kid, when I'd done something that really tickled her. She sounded so proud. I inferred that a "back rack" was someone you could lean on, someone who took care of family, and the more she said it, the richer the word became. It also meant you were a winner. It meant you were a real sport. Sometimes it meant you had chutzpah and pulled one over on them and got away with it. It took me years to realize it was spelled "Bachrach" and it was her maiden name, but by then the term seemed better than a Nobel Prize. Which is why I changed my name to Bachrach, to please her and officially become myself, when I moved to Paris. I took her name, even though I knew by then what Bachrach really meant.

While all stable families resemble one another, to paraphrase Tolstoy, all unstable families are unstable in their own way. A few of the Bachrachs rose to and fell from such high places that they could have invented gravity. The family patriarch, who came to America from Poland in 1898, was the most exalted rabbi in New England in the twenties and thirties and was considered a genius. He was the chief rabbi of Rhode Island, leading the righteous in prayer, interpreting the kabbalah, resolving religious disputes. At home, he stayed mostly in his study davening, his head in a prayer book and his back, apparently, to everything else.

His nine children were intelligent and well educated, but it was the Depression, and they were broke. All of them married, though not all of them multiplied, and then they set out on their own. But nearly every one came back to Providence the way they had left, penniless and in trouble. They were not standard issue, and there isn't a normal story in the bunch. They were clever and ambitious. They were imaginative and unscrupulous. They were driven and unstable. They courted danger and took risks. At times, they behaved like a pack of sociopaths. Yet while they were busy screwing everyone around them, they were fanatical about protecting one another. Whoever was up took care of the ones who were down—Bachrach family values.

My grandmother loved to brag about her sisters and brothers, how smart they were, how "swell." Her eyes would light up when she described Mora's private Pullman car and the fortune she made in her boiler room. "Does that mean she's in the heating business?" I asked. "No heat." My grandmother laughed, launching me into twenty questions. I could never figure it out. "It's a bucket shop," she finally told me. "What kind of buckets?" I asked. That made her roar. Apparently, there were no buckets, either.

Her brothers were "real big shots" in Washington and the elder one, Larry, was "a gen-u-ine VIP." He played poker in the White House—he was "like this" with President Harding. In fact, she told me, he was the president's personal "procurer," which I took to mean that Larry kept the pantry stocked in the family quarters. He used to joke that the president sent him to the U.S. Treasury when he was losing at cards. Then Larry flashed his trademark gold cuff links, perfect facsimiles of the Treasury Building. So maybe Larry *wasn't* joking. When the Harding administration was investigated for bribery during the Teapot Dome scandal, Larry was "the *only* federal judge to go to jail." My grandmother recounted this fact proudly—the implication being that the *other* federal judges weren't nearly as important.

Her little brother, Billy, was another ambiguous source of pride. He came to visit us once when he was "on leave," but I have no memory of his face. I've heard that's a characteristic of spies—they learn to blend in and be invisible. An unremarkable man of about fifty, in a nondescript dark suit, he stood with his back to me in a cloud of cigarette smoke at the stove, flipping "Uncle Billy eggs" with one hand and Lucky Strikes with the other. Then he went back to Panama to take care of a *big* assignment at the canal, something *very* important. My grandmother hinted he was an assassin.

This is what it meant to be a Bachrach.

But the most famous person in the family wasn't a Bachrach at all; it was Nana's husband, "Young Montreal," the man I thought was my grandfather. Monty was a champion featherweight boxer in the twenties, standing five foot three and weighing in at 108 pounds. In over a hundred professional bouts, he was knocked out only once. He was "a clever puncher, with superb footwork and the ability to withstand punishment," according to his clippings from the *New York Times*. Once, before a fight, he broke his wrist after going a round with a hot stove he'd hit in anger, but he taped up his hand, went into the ring, and knocked his opponent out in four rounds. He drew big crowds into Madison Square Garden and took home big purses, but he gambled his winnings away at the dog track, abetted by Nana and accompanied by her nephew, the track accountant, who fled the country after he was indicted for embezzling.

What kind of people embezzle from the mob?

In one of *her stories*, Nana confessed hiding all night in the attic with Monty's loaded pistol, afraid somebody was coming to get her. She'd been "watching some money," she told me, and it had disappeared "just like that." "How do you watch money?" I asked her. "And if you're watching it, how does it disappear?" "The track" was her answer. Then she smiled. "I loved the dogs."

Monty had to leave town for a while in the twenties because his pool hall was torched and his home was dynamited "a little," for reasons that remain a mystery to this day. By the time I was born, he had retired from the ring to a bar stool downtown on Steeple Street, where he passed his afternoons drinking beer in the company of erstwhile admirers who could be counted on to root "Hey, Champ!" whenever he staggered through the bar door.

During the Depression, when Lola was a child, Monty and Leah couldn't make ends meet, or couldn't make them stretch past the dog track, so they moved in with Leah's father, the rabbi, who lived in a three-story Victorian tenement on North Main Street. The plaque in his peeling front hallway recognized the home as A GIFT OF THE JEWISH PEOPLE. In those days, the Jewish people provided room but not board, and they didn't pay much of a salary. The chief rabbi was a pauper who earned actual money only at Passover, when delis hired him to stamp Coca-Cola bottles *Kosher L'Pesach*.

Leah's sisters and brothers sent money when they could—whenever, I guess, they weren't in the slammer. And to pay the milkman, or anyone else who wouldn't take hot S&H Green Stamps from Monty, Leah rented out a room on the third floor of the house—the rabbi's house—to "Madame Dorée," one of my mother's role models growing up, the girlfriend of another "gen-u-ine VIP," Raymond Patriarca. My grandmother didn't have to tell me who "Uncle Ray" was, since anyone who could read a newspaper knew he was "Providence Public Enemy #1"—the local head of the Mafia and a candidate for the slammer.

These were the stories Nana liked to tell, and the exploits of her band of merry miscreants were bedtime fare whenever Lola was "away." But when Lola got home, this whole generation of history was consigned to oblivion—all my mother wanted to talk about was her grandfather, the brilliant rabbi. "He was the most brilliant man in all of New England" was how *her* tale began. It was a heavily censored version of our ancestral psychodrama, and if Nana was our Homer, Lola was our Rose Mary Woods.

In my mother's expurgated family history, no criminals appear. Instead, Rabbi Bachrach stars as the Spiritual Leader of the Jews. Lola recounted his legend in book-length paragraphs at compressed speed, fluttering from one anecdote to another like a hummingbird. How often she'd told me that he was a genius, "the most brilliant man in all of New England," the *chief* rabbi. His judgment "rivaled King Solomon's." His lineage traced back to 1630, to the first Orthodox rabbi in Eastern Europe. How many times had I listened to the chronicle of his funeral procession—when Lola had just turned twelve—the horse-drawn cortege that carried his coffin across Providence as all the shuls threw open their doors to honor his passing body.

But once his funeral was over and his body was in the ground, the view from the street was about as close as the Rabbi's offspring ever got to a shul again—except for Lola—and the reason was something they all referred to as "The Rabbi's Troubles" and rarely referred to at all when there were children in the room. I recognized the phrase and the loud silences that accompanied it as the big rug under which everything was buried, and "The Rabbi's Troubles" turned me into Nancy Drew.

How could this genius—who died nearly a decade before I was born—have been such a laudable public figure but such a lamentable role model? Why was his house such a great place for an Italian mobster to hide his French mistress? Why was his eldest son a jailed judge, his youngest an assassin at large, and his middle daughter running a bucket shop that had no buckets? How did this man who penetrated the sacred mysteries of the kabbalah overlook the hoods in his household? Didn't he smell the liquor on their breath and the dynamite on their fingers? That's what Nancy Drew wanted to know.

As soon as I was old enough and no one was looking, I placed an ad in the *Rhode Island Jewish Herald* for anyone who might remember the rabbi, who died in 1939, and I got one anonymous call from a curmudgeon, who hung up after enticing me with an unintentional hint: "Whattaya gotta go diggin' that stuff up for?" And so I spent a week in the Providence Public Library digging through decades of microfilm and found "The Rabbi's Troubles" on the front page in 1924, month after month, during Prohibition.

At a time when there were stills on every corner, when America was a tipsy seesaw with a flask of booze at its fulcrum, when it was well known that an appreciable number of congressmen were drunk on their ass on the floor of the House and Senate and Uncle Larry said there'd been enough alcohol at President Harding's poker games to embalm his whole cabinet, that's when Rabbi Bachrach—who had a right to sell sacramental wine to his congregation—was arrested and tried for bootlegging. And after his mistrial, he was retried.

Why him? He was the first clergyman in America whose right to sell sacramental wine was challenged. But the feds had decided to test the religious "loophole" to the dry laws, and when they looked around for a suitable defendant, the famous rabbi was ideal. He was more convictable than a priest—and more arrestable, too—since he'd refused to pay protection money even *after* his warehouse was torched.

It was all in the Providence newspapers—the photo of the rabbi's arrest outside the shul and his mug shot, in which he was wearing a yarmulke; the description of him leaning on his ivory cane as he walked into the Providence courthouse accompanied by the most famous man in town, his son-in-law, Young Montreal.

I read the fed's trumped-up charges and the rabbi's countercharges, including his accusation, backed up by witnesses, that the feds had tried to extort money from him. He may have been "the most brilliant man in all of New England," but Rabbi Bachrach forgot the most important lesson he'd learned in Bialystok—that extortion is the prelude to a pogrom.

Out on bail and brandishing his principles, the chief rabbi countersued the federal government in 1925, arguing that his constitutional rights were being violated. The following week, he was arrested again, this time for marrying a couple before putting his official stamp on their wedding license. This particular violation was so egregious that he was dragged from his home in his ceremonial robes on the Sabbath and paraded in handcuffs before waiting photographers.

That night, he slept in a jail cell next to a pair of twenty-year-old Mafia thugs—Angelo Tucci and Salvatore D'Angelo—who were accused of murdering a "colleague" on a wharf and throwing his body parts into the Providence River. The arrest docket identified their nationality as American, although they'd been born in Sicily a few years before, while the nationality of the rabbi, who'd lived in America for almost three decades, was identified only as "Jew."

And because Yahweh failed, repeatedly, to come to the rescue of a man made in His image, the rabbi's offspring traded the insecurity of the synagogue for the serendipity of the streets. There, despite their old-world upbringing and Ivy League educations, they shared the woozy values of the times.

If the cops were coming for the Jews, they might as well be guilty.

. . .

At eighty-two, Aunt Flossie—one of the few law-abiding siblings in a generation of small scoundrels—lives in a nursing home in downtown Providence, where she is drugged or deeply depressed, or both. No one ever acknowledged that she was Lola's real mother—we pretended we didn't have a clue, even though the air was denser than a black hole when Flossie was around, and everyone knew what happened when she took over Lola's thinking.

Ben figured it out as a teenager, suffering through a brief stay in Flossie's apartment in Flushing, a malodorous walk-up in a ramshackle building. The first clue was the whorehouse piano she'd bought so he'd have something to practice on during the three days and seven hours he would be there. The next hint was three oil portraits, one of each of us, that had disappeared mysteriously from our living room several years earlier and now hung brazenly over her couch.

After Flossie went to her job transcribing medical records, Ben "happened upon" (read: ransacked) her memorabilia, and in a leather box in her cluttered desk, he found Lola's birth certificate, clipped to a Saint Christopher medal. Flossie was listed as the mother, and the father was someone Ben had never even heard of. He didn't say a word to anyone at the time, and it took him ten years to tell me.

He was staying at Aunt Flossie's while he performed at the 1964 World's Fair. After winning a million talent contests, he'd been named "Mr. Junior Rhode Island," and he was debuting with a symphony in the Rhode Island State Pavilion—an official prodigy at fourteen. It wasn't just how cute he was—small, with silky blond hair—and it wasn't just his talent at the keyboard. It was the back story—the fact that he played with nine and a half fingers. Even Mozart needed ten!

Our fourteen-year-old wunderkind strode out onto an enormous stage at the World's Fair after a tense day at Aunt Flossie's reconstructing his family tree, with hundreds of people in the audience, maybe a thousand, and he was standing tall to make the most of the thick pink soles under his white bucks, just as he heard the announcer snip three years off his age and introduce him over the loudspeaker as "little eleven-year-old Benny." A well-played *Rhapsody in Blue*, no small feat for a teenager, would be even more newsworthy for an eleven-year-old, wouldn't it? Especially one whose thumb started life as a lobster claw. This charade was perpetrated by his mother, who probably imagined Sol Hurok in the audience, while she was perpetrating a second charade with "Aunt" Flossie.

Ben promptly gave the worst performance of his life. And in the car on the ride home, he began to wonder whether his so-called talent came not from our tap-dancing "grandmother's" admirable self-taught honky-tonk, but, instead, from the unmusical *qwerty* typing of "Aunt" Flossie, medical stenographer *ordinaire*, his real flesh and blood.

A few years later, when Ben and Helen were teenagers and I was in college, Lola took them to a dentist they'd never seen before, even though they didn't have an appointment and there was nothing wrong with their teeth. His was the name on Lola's birth certificate. They sat in his waiting room and watched Lola go into his private office. When the door opened briefly, they glimpsed a man with red hair behind a desk. Lola, in overdrive, had picked this day to ask Red, who'd never once acknowledged her, if he wanted to meet his grandchildren. But he didn't leave his office, and he didn't even glance into the waiting room, and eventually she came out and drove them home.

From the time I was old enough to read, Aunt Flossie wrote me exorbitant letters full of advice, and she was curious about me in a way I couldn't fathom. Her envelopes overflowed with wrinkled clippings on the power of Christian Science to heal warts, cankers, depression, gout, acne, menstrual cramps, and cancer. This was a peculiar preoccupation for a medical stenographer, especially one with an Orthodox Jewish background. But what's clear is that she'd inherited the rabbi's gene for religiosity and passed it on to Lola.

Sooner or later, we're going to have to face Aunt Flossie.

Helen selects a stiff carnation bouquet from Lola's growing floral collection, and we head downtown to Highbridge Nursing Home.

"How much should we tell her about the accident?" I ask Helen on the way, imagining how little it would take to blow the lid off Pandora's box.

"The truth," she replies—an option that hadn't even occurred to me.

"Why don't we just answer her questions," Ben suggests, the only one among us who's laissez-faire.

Controlling Aunt Flossie is probably beyond our combined talents anyway, since the Rhode Island chapter of the American Psychiatric Association has already failed at the task.

At reception, the odor of disinfectant could control malaria in a Third World country. But on the top floor, amid a still life of bedpans, the smell approaches ripe Camembert. Highbridge may be as clean and pleasant as a nursing home can be, but it smells like the last stop in purgatory.

Flossie is in a bed by a window, staring blankly, but she recognizes us right away. Her resemblance to Lola is indisputable—the same skittish eyes, the hyperintelligent stare, the jutting overbite, the frizzy Valkyrie curls. The mirror beside her bed confirms my own unfortunate likeness. Our polite small talk is drowned out by an invisible roommate, who's moaning from a bed behind a drawn curtain, and so Ben puts Flossie in a wheelchair and rolls her down to the empty Social Room, which is decorated with old movie posters. There, in an attempt to be upbeat and probably to avoid conversation, he plays the "Black Key Etude," a short, happy confection of chords and speed, on a piano that hasn't been tuned since Roosevelt was in the White House. The poster hanging above him features Barbara Stanwyck in *Stella Dallas*.

> Stella realizes that her daughter
> will go further in life without her . . .
> but the sacrifice is shattering.

Twenty uncomfortable minutes later, when the aroma of creamed corn begins to overpower the Pine-Sol, we wheel Flossie back to her room. She never asks about Mort, and only when Ben has tucked her back into bed does she inquire about Lola.

"She can't visit right now," he says.

There's no reaction.

"Because she's in the hospital," Helen adds—unnecessarily, I think.

But Flossie doesn't flinch, having heard that alibi before, no doubt. Maybe she thinks Helen means the usual hospital, the sanitarium. Still, she could have inquired. But since there's no follow-up, I make a run for the door, and after a few minutes, Ben and Helen bring up the rear.

The painfully cheerful nurse at reception signs us out. "Would you like to make any changes in your instructions?" she asks, with a baffling grin.

"What instructions," I ask, wondering if DO NOT RESUSCITATE is inscribed in Flossie's chart.

"Next of kin? We wondered if your mother is still Florence's next of kin."

Lola hadn't volunteered to be next of kin—the designation was strictly a function of attrition. After Nana died, there was no one else in line. Evidently, this nurse has heard about the boat accident and wants the final death toll—to see who should be notified *in the event of*. Now it's my turn.

"Call me," I volunteer. "I'm next."

Thus do I rise to the occasion of my primogeniture and accept my inheritance, Aunt Flossie.

SIX

Mal de Mère

After escaping unscathed from Aunt Flossie, we find more huge bouquets outside Lola's apartment door, including a white carnation horseshoe on a plastic easel, the kind that belongs in a Mafia movie. It's a typical statement of excess from the mayor of Providence, Buddy Cianci, whose previous awards to Lola include a wall full of proclamations and plaques for her charitable work. Theirs is a mutual-admiration society. Lola says she'd "swear in court he has a heart of gold." And she may have to, since Buddy's been accused of assaulting his wife's boyfriend with a cigarette, an ashtray, and a fireplace poker. He's the most recent in a long line of golden-hearted thugs who remind Lola of her dear old uncle Ray, "Providence Public Enemy #1."

Once I get through the botanical shrine, I hear the phone ringing (the answering machine, guess what, does not work). It's Lola's psychiatrist, Frank Blitzer, and he needs to speak urgently to *Dr.* Hornstein. He makes "*Dr.*" sound like *the man of the house*, so even though Helen and I both have Ph.D.'s, I know he's calling for the male lead.

Having "managed" Lola for five years, Dr. Blitzer has a couple of her breakdowns already under his belt. Unencumbered by sensitivity, his only advice to me over the years has been to "be a good girl, because that's all your mother really wants," from which I inferred that my sassiness as a child and bitchiness as an adolescent were all that stood between her and mental health. He's calling now from her bedside at Our Lady by the Sea, like a war correspondent reporting from the front, to alert Dr. Hornstein that "the patient is under a lot of stress."

Ben thanks him profusely for this insight, rolling his eyes, holding the phone so Helen and I can listen in, and he agrees that, yes, "stress certainly is contraindicated in this patient's case." We'll get right on it.

"Mrs. Hornstein's difficulties always seem to be precipitated by life stresses," Blitzer intones, which sounds vaguely like Mort's "too much pressure" theory. "She hasn't accepted her husband's death. She talks like someone coming off a drunk, and she's even striking up a breezy social life in the hospital."

My mother's never been to a hospital she couldn't organize into social clubs with ginger ale happy hours, but Dr. Blitzer thinks this is "the tip of the mania iceberg," and he pronounces her "mildly euphoric."

To wit, he's already upped her lithium.

Blitzer thinks this is mania? One business letter drafted on her deathbed? One posthumous porn story? This is nothing. This is *shock*.

Mania is hiring a couple of strippers as luncheon entertainment at the Ladies' Home for the Aged.

Mania is broiling and freezing thirty dozen chicken wings in Catalina sauce "to get a jump on condolence meals" for friends who aren't feeling well but aren't dead yet. ("Who's gonna notice the freezer burn?")

Mania is epic poetry—and I've heard just one rhyme since she regained consciousness. Only when she describes Mort's death in heroic couplets will *I* call it mania.

Besides, the hospital's chief of staff says Lola's doing well enough to be released in a few days. True, her gait is slow and her balance is tipsy, but he predicts "a complete recovery." Yes, he noted the psych warnings in her chart, but other than lithium, "what is one to do, really, with her psychiatric history?"

That's what I want to know.

Gathered in Lola's den on Friday night, a week after the accident, my siblings and I are armed with frozen Smirnoff, coping with death by toasting to life—*L'Chaim*—and knocking back our Shabbos shots like Russians in winter.

"What would Caesar do?" Ben asks, reminding us (once again) that he won the Latin prize at Classical High.

"Caesar divided Gaul into three parts," Helen replies. She went to Classical, too.

How convenient, Ben points out, since there are three parts of the problem called Lola. Then our little Caesar divides our mater up, giving himself the mammoth medical heaping, granting Helen the sizable psychiatric slice, and awarding me the paltry portion he calls "financial."

Everyone agrees. *L'Chaim.*

But I haven't gotten off easy, Ben continues, because along with my meager portion comes the first watch—since if he doesn't get back to Bellevue, the emergency room will hemorrhage, and if Helen doesn't get back to signing with her deaf patients, their fingers will atrophy. Whereas if I don't return to Paris, the French will just keep on masking their sweat with cologne, and I'm getting paid wherever I am.

So I stay.

When they leave on Sunday night, I have phantom pains in my umbilical cord. Or maybe it's the start of an ulcer.

The first few days of my watch, "the old woman in the hospital bed" holds court in a succession of colorful bed jackets brought to her in beautifully wrapped boxes by friends. The mayor comes by with more flowers. Soap operas stream in from the nurses' station "like sands through the hourglass."

Lola never mentions Mort.

"Your mother is holding up so well," her friends remark, rotating in and out.

"She's so cheerful, so breezy, so strong."

Dr. Blitzer has put his finger on the problem with *that*.

After visiting hours, I settle into her apartment alone, armed with sharp pencils and an adding machine, deconstructing my father's finances—his byzantine labyrinth of "private holding companies." I've found several empty shells that "hold" almost nothing—their primary assets being stationery, business cards, and checkbooks linked by check kiting. There's no will, although that's a moot point, but his insurance policy will pay double for *accidental death*, which my recently hired death consultant swears Mort will qualify for. Add it up and Lola has bingo—with juggling, she'll be able to stay in this apartment. Juggling is how she and Mort stayed here this long.

After a few days, I get to the bottom of the bills and tackle the mail, and that's when I spot an envelope addressed to Lola in her own handwriting, postmarked the day of the accident. Its return address is the marina where Mort's lethal weapon was docked. She must have mailed it just before they walked the gangplank, and I rip it open so fast, I get paper cuts on both hands.

You want a day that's just outstanding?
Come July 4th to Folly's Landing.
We guarantee a day that's smooth,
If there are whitecaps, we won't move.
For everyone with mal de mère,
We'll take a cruise that goes nowhere!

The printed invitation, which in hindsight reads like a death threat, must have reached her friends when they got home from Mort's funeral—inviting them to a party whose prequel killed the host. How many of them would have been exterminated on a cold evening, sipping vodka gimlets in the galley with "the Captain," after he'd battened down the hatches and cranked up his generator? "So clean, you could eat off it," he liked to brag.

Thank God, they must be saying. *If only.*

It's beginning to dawn on me, now that the Captain's gone down with his ship, that the nausea I endured whenever I boarded, the endless urgent queue at the head, did not come entirely from the whitecaps, or even the nightcaps. Nor can Lola's cholesterol festival explain it—those bacon-wrapped chicken livers went down without complaint on land. "Mal de mère" was how Lola explained it, brushing it off as seasickness but misspelling it—and inadvertently coining a phrase that translates literally as "mother sickness." But that doesn't explain it, either.

I puked in rough seas or smooth, fed or fasting, whether Mort smoked his stogie or abstained, and regardless of the guest list. And I wasn't the only one. The boat's salon, its saloon, was just above the generator, Mr. Fix It's pride and joy, the aging hunk of pitted red iron lurking within the deathtrap.

Which has just taken its final cruise to nowhere.

. . . .

"Make sure she gets plenty of fresh air," the head nurse advises me when I check Lola out of Our Lady. These are my only instructions.

"Okay," I say blankly, grateful for any suggestions.

Lola, seated in her wheelchair, gets a standing ovation from her doctors and nurses as she signs her discharge form, and it's like watching the president sign a bill into law. Except that Lola makes it look like really hard work, pushing that ballpoint pen across the page as though there's a lot of resistance and she needs to give it a good shove to make it cooperate. Her hand is shaking from a tremor I'm trying to ignore, having been promised "a complete recovery" by the chief of staff.

She waits for someone to tell her what to do next, and so I take the pen and paper from her hand, and as I pass them to the head nurse, I see that where Lola was supposed to have signed her own name, she's written "Mort Hornstein." I'm not sure what to make of this—whether it's just a slip of the hand or a portent of schizophrenia. I say nothing, and no one else seems to notice.

The head nurse says, "Good-bye, Lola, good luck" (and she certainly means it), and that's when she expresses her faith in proper ventilation.

"Fresh air," she repeats, "lots of fresh air."

A bright smile accompanies her benediction, while the rest of her face reveals the effort of the gesture.

The smile is really all she can offer—that's what her eyes tell me. Other than lithium, there is no prescription to fill, no medical guidance to follow, no social worker to direct me, and no personal advice. There are also no precedents, since the hospital staff's entire experience with carbon-monoxide poisoning consists of the man I buried a week ago and the woman I'm about to wheel out the door.

My job is to help my mother recover from a gas overdose and adapt to widowhood, but I have no idea what to do once we leave the parking lot. I will certainly limit her daily exposure to toxic fumes. I will shield her from secondhand cigarette smoke, buses, and gas ovens. I will lay out her lithium in the morning and make sure that she swallows. And there will be absolutely no boats. But beyond that, I haven't a clue.

Taking Lola home is bound to put her in touch with reality, with Mort's postmortem, to make her "shock" evolve into something more predictably lunatic. A few days, maybe a week, and it'll hit her. I'll be her monitor. I'll be her chef, chauffeur, coiffeuse, and caretaker. I'll be all that stands between her and "the worst that could happen." If I get lucky, she'll have her breakdown after my watch. But if it happens during, Helen will take over. Anyway, this is our plan.

Belting Lola into the passenger seat of her blue Buick, I lower the convertible top to aerate her—nurse's orders.

"That's nice," she says—vacuously—as I weave around cars and trucks so she won't be downwind from exhaust. While the breeze is exactly what the head nurse ordered, as her hairdresser, I'm horrified, having spent the last half hour teasing her hair to make her look cheered up, so I could cheer myself up. I molded and sprayed her red beehive into a confection that in this humidity feels like cotton candy, and by the time we get to her apartment in Cranston, the muggy breeze has turned her into a troll doll.

Her next-door neighbor, Mrs. Freedman, comes running out in a terry-cloth bathrobe, waving a dish towel, to deliver condolences. She doesn't let on that my mother is an eyesore. Maybe that's what she expected.

"I was so sorry to hear about your loss," she says, referring to my late father as though he's a misplaced accessory that may eventually turn up.

"That's nice," Lola says, holding still for a bereavement hug, but looking puzzled.

When Mrs. Freedman walks away, Lola whispers to me, "Is Daddy dead?"

"Yes, he died on the boat."

"Oh. I thought I dreamed it."

She pauses, then repeats, "On the boat?"

"Yes, on the boat."

"That's too bad. Is the boat okay?"

Inside, I throw open the windows and turn on the ceiling fans even though the central air-conditioning is on high. Lola asks for cartons, and after rummaging through the trash room, I come up with a dozen. In two hours, with her customary zeal, she removes all of Mort's belongings from his closets and drawers, calls Goodwill, and makes herself a stiff drink. It's not even teatime and she's medicated herself with a fistful of scotch and taken to her bed with her cat, who probably has a proper name but, like all his predecessors, regardless of gender, is called "Pussy."

SEVEN

The Undertow

A colony of aphids is making a feast of the dwindling flowers, spinning white webs of decay where chlorophyll once thrived. Lola's been home for a week and my solo grip on the botanical chores is slipping. Fresh bouquets arrive daily, and I stack them up in front of old ones that are withering, unable to dispose of anything permanently, even if it's terminal.

Despite the hospital's prognosis of "a complete recovery," which I hope will kick in any day now, Lola seems to be withering, too. Instead of her customary hysteria, for which I've steeled myself, she's impenetrably dull—increasingly flat, dense, cotton-headed, listless, irritable, and unresponsive to everything but my French cooking.

Between meals and naps, her friends drop by, but she hasn't said a word about Mort since she packed up what was left of him and shipped it off to Goodwill. She hasn't said a word about much of anything else, either. With no sign of the mania that Blitzer misdiagnosed—no Olympic talking or rhyming, no shopping frenzy, no biblical code or Copernican revolution—I'm sticking with my diagnosis of *shock*, with an escalating overlay of depression. But I'm not reassured to see that her seesaw is on the downswing, since gravity has never been her friend.

While I excel at grocery shopping and cooking—and this is certainly one of the tastiest shivas anyone's ever been to—I'm a failure at daughterly companionship. I skate along my mother's dull surface, and I haven't once asked her how she's *really* feeling. I'm too scared even to think about it. One of my lifelong principles is to avoid getting anywhere near the vortex at the center of the universe.

One warm day, I take Lola to Narragansett Beach, where we had a little summer cottage in the mid-fifties. How many times had she taken all three of us to the ocean when we were kids? She schlepped a beach umbrella and a cooler full of tuna sandwiches and a blanket and a beach chair and a book—four books—across the hot white sand, three in tow, to get to the water's edge so we could dig for sand crabs.

We bring no book this time. We walk on the beach, and Lola gazes vaguely at the horizon, a fuzzy look on her face. Her gait is lumbering, tipsy, more than the sand can account for. I buy her a pair of flip-flops because she complains that the sand is too hot.

Up ahead, two men kneel at the water's edge, searching for something under the breaking waves, signaling to the children around them to stay back.

"What did you lose?" I call out.

"A knife, we lost a jackknife."

They turn toward us, and one of them makes a "Stay back"

gesture with his hands. Lola sees the commotion but not the warning, and she moves faster into the action.

"Watch out. You'll step on the knife, lady," one of them yells.

I see it coming. Even they see it coming. Oh no, please no, don't let my mother stab herself in the foot. Who is going to save her, who will put a tourniquet on her dripping sandy shank, and which one of these men will carry her off the beach in his arms?

"Mom, stop. You need shoes! You need shoes!"

"I am wearing shoes," she yells back, pointing to her flip-flops, just as she steps directly on the blade. I watch its tip pierce the rubber.

That night, she keeps her foot elevated in front of the TV while I run around to satisfy her frequent needs—more juice, another cookie, a different channel—and her ongoing question: "What is Ben's phone number? What is Ben's phone number? What is Ben's phone number?"

I perform constant, endless chores in service of her needy inactivity, to make up for how useless I was on the scene. Her wound was superficial—she hobbled off the beach on her own—but I was so exhausted by my vision of disaster, by my mounting self-propelled hysteria, that I nearly fainted. I swooned, like some twenties ingenue. I pretended I wanted to examine the bottom of her foot. The truth was that I needed to lie down—fast. The sun was glaring, the air was dense, and I was woozy. I felt my knees buckle first, and then my body gave in to its weight. "Let me look at your foot," I mumbled as I fell, trying to cover up my asinine performance and catch my breath. I wanted to lie in the sand until these two strangers could come to my rescue and get me back on my feet.

. . .

Tonight, our social life is bound to improve, because Lola's cousins, Irving and Esther, have invited us out to dinner at Edgemere Country Club, Lola's land-based social life. The clubhouse is in Massachusetts, twenty minutes out of town, an imposing white manor with huge columns like Tara's, sitting amid eighteen holes of a gorgeously manicured golf course. As Lola makes her way up the wide staircase to the main floor, everyone wants to squeeze her hand, and the members line up to whisper condolences, with their good intentions fluttering around her like confetti at a ticker-tape parade.

Irving and Esther are waiting for us in the bar at the top of the stairs. At seventy, she is erect and big-boned, with massive waves of white hair and a gentle smile. She's sharp as the day she earned her Phi Beta Kappa key from Pembroke, and she's the only one of my mother's female relatives I consider certifiably sane. For this, Irving likes to take all the credit, bragging that he kept her away from her family—Lola's family and mine—the Bachrachs.

When we get to the table, we order a second round. It being happy hour, the drinks are robust, and Irving is setting the pace with martinis. A retired furniture salesman, he looks like the Cookie Monster but is as voluble as Big Bird, a raconteur with dirt on everybody and a memory that stretches back to the Rabbi's Troubles. He has no fear of talking now that I've dug up the facts, although he stonewalled for years.

"The rabbi was framed," he's telling our table, although I'm the only one who's interested. "The feds set him up."

"The rabbi was a great man, Irving," Esther says, nudging him under the table to shut up.

Lola doesn't seem to notice, since she's slurping the straw of her second mai tai and stabbing the pink paper parasol with the green plastic sword. She's been reserved all evening, as she has been all week, but now that she's sucked her second drink dry, she turns animated, interrupting Irving in the middle of a rabbi joke. She seems to have something very pressing to tell us.

"Baw rawsh par i keef," she says, and smiles. Actually, she blushes.

Irving cups his ear to hear her better. "*Huh?* What did Lola say?"

"I think she has a parakeet," Esther tells him, looking to me for confirmation, her own ears bulging with hearing aids.

"*What* parakeet?" I ask Lola, since if she has one, it hasn't been fed since I got to town.

"Dtt chmt rck," she replies, coughing up phlegmy hair balls of sound.

"I can't *hear* her. What's Lola saying?" Irving says too loudly. The people at the next table stop talking and look over. "*What's* the bird's name?"

"Crk ftch."

I stare at Lola.

She grins. She beams. She looks like little Shirley Temple, all innocence and tight curls.

And then she expectorates more vowel-less clumps.

"Tch pft pr frmck."

Turning to me for an explanation, Esther's face shifts gradually from confusion to embarrassment to alarm. *Why is your mother speaking in tongues?* she seems to be asking.

I do not have an answer. This is new ground, even for my mother.

Once dinner arrives, Lola works her way through an inch-thick slab of cow, then picks up the rib and finishes it off. A mouthful of gristle takes the pressure off conversation, and there is no more gibberish. Irving leads us gently back into jokes and small talk, Lola stops talking altogether, and we all pretend we haven't turned up in an Ionesco play. What's the alternative?

I wipe medium-rare meat off my mother's chin and rush

everyone through the make-your-own sundaes so we can get outside and bulk up on fresh air.

"Nch ng znt," she remarks when we get home. Then she goes to her room and shuts her door.

This is not going well.

"She shouldn't be drinking," Ben tells me over the phone that night. "No alcohol. Period. And maybe you should switch to Evian, too."

In my dream, an old woman is lying in a hospital bed. She wants a wine cooler in her room. She has to have it. *So what* if she's in intensive care? *That's* what she wants. So I get a meeting with the hospital review board to present her case, and they're beginning to lean my way, but then Ben shows up as a witness for the prosecution and testifies that "the whole thing is futile." I turn on the light to write the dream down, thinking it's Lola in the hospital bed and trying to figure out what's futile, but by the time I locate a pen, I've begun to think that *I'm* the old woman, and that I should have ordered wine with dinner, instead of a second round.

Outside my door, squeaky floorboards announce that Lola's awake, roaming around in the middle of the night. This is not a good development. Insomnia has always been the first whiff of her mania—before dawn, she could read a book or two *(libromania)* and then turn epistolary *(graphomania)*. She'd write away for useless things she'd seen in magazines, emptying my father's wallet before he woke up *(fritter-o-philia)*. She wrote to lawyers, asking them to sue people who'd wronged us (the periodical salesman, the camp director, the nature counselor). And because some of her envelopes were addressed incorrectly, intentionally perhaps, they were returned to our house. I tore one open, and cash flew out. *Dear Sir, Enclosed is a retainer of twenty-five dollars to sue my husband for divorce.* I pocketed the money and threw the note away before my father got home. I made a habit of that.

Her letter fixation waxed and waned, but when it was over, it was followed by periods when prose would simply not suffice. Then, in the flush of *metromania*, she turned into the whirling dervish of poetry—composing limericks, sonnets, jingles, and musical parodies. And she performed the best of them at breakfast.

I got a right to sing the blues
Can't pay my mortgage or my dues,
I got a right to sing the blues,
'Cause we're headed to the
Poooooorhouse.

But tonight, after our nightmare at the club, there's no singing, no whirling, and neither poetry nor prose. Tonight there's no speech at all, not even the ancient Celtic she was fluent in at dinner. Lola is in the small hallway outside her room, staring at the ceiling, bug-eyed, looking frantic but holding still, as though she's been abandoned in a foreign country and doesn't know what language to scream in.

"Mom? It's not even three o'clock."

She looks *toward* me, but not exactly at me. It's as though there's a scrim between us, or she's unable to focus, or there's a jamming device in her head.

She says nothing.

"Want some coffee?" I ask.

She hums the Nescafe jingle. *Hm hm hm, hm hm hm hm hm hmmm.*

Humming must mean yes.

On our way to the kitchen, she snuggles up to me like a magnet. I ask her to sit at the table while I work at the sink, but a second later I sense her coming up behind me again. I feel her warm breath on the back of my neck, and it makes my hair stand on end. When I back up, we collide. When I turn around, we're nose-to-nose. She sidles up against me at the stove while the water is coming to a boil, and I apologize and push her away so I can breathe. But I can't detach her. She's stuck to me like a barnacle. And she's still humming.

I sense the moist heat of her body in the clammy space between us. I taste the coffee-flavored air she exhales. I *feel* her stomach growl. And now that all our gases are getting mixed together, I remember I should be ventilating her more. But I can't get to the window, because she's wedged up against me at the sink and is feeling around me for something—I don't know what—and then the silverware in the sink starts rattling like there's an earthquake as the garbage grinder growls into action even though I never touched it, and the sudden noise and vibration scare the shit out of me.

"*What the hell did you do that for?*" I push her away and switch the grinder off.

"What the hell what the hell what the hell what the hell what the hell . . ." she says.

Time stops flowing and snaps.

Lola leans over my shoulder, repeating the words *what the hell* like an echo chamber, staring into the sink, beaming at the water flowing down the drain, mesmerized by the miracle of—what, indoor plumbing?

I leave the water running—what's the harm?—and go to clear the table. If I sponge off the table and do the dishes, if I keep pushing through this new warp in the center of the universe and just act normal, everything will turn out to be normal. Unless it turns out to be a dream. Which would be fine, too.

"*Grrrrr grrrrrr grrrrrrrrrrrr.*"

"Mom, please, I'm begging you. Will you stop that?"

"Stop that stop that stop that stop that stop that . . ."

I open the kitchen window. Maybe we need more air.

After another chorus of "stop that stop that," she stops that.

"Why don't I just fix you a nice breakfast?" I say. Like I'm Betty Crocker. "How about pancakes?"

"Pancakes pancakes pancakes . . ."

It doesn't take me a minute to stop talking altogether.

While the pancakes are cooking and my back is turned, Lola starts *grrrr*-ing again and not a second later the grinder roars back into action. And then, in verrry sloooooow motion, I see her reach into the sink and aim for the disposal, in a trance, like Alice following the rabbit down the hole, only the hole is a meat grinder.

Adrenaline launches me across the room, and I yank her hands away from the churning blades and press her fingers tightly between mine to see if they're leaking, then count all the way to ten before I start weeping. My mother doesn't notice that I'm weeping because she's too busy reaching around me to turn on the grinder again.

"*Grrrr grrrrr grrrrrrrrr.*"

I'm in way over my head here.

After dawn, I start dialing her shrink, Dr. Blitzer, knowing it's too early for him to be in the office but unable to resist the urge to take some action, however pointless. In my mother's home, the shrink's number is posted on the refrigerator, above the fire department's. Last year, when she was visiting me in Paris, I had to go to London overnight, so I put a friend's phone number on my fridge, in case Lola needed anything while I was gone. "Is your friend a psychiatrist?" she asked.

"Doctor's office," a sleepy, crabby voice says after a dozen rings.

"Is he in, please?" I'm already pleading.

"*Who*, is *who* in?"

"Dr. Blitzer."

"Not before nine."

"Does he call in for messages?"

"I can't answer that; we're just an answering service. Is this an emergency?"

This is a very good question. Last night, my mother was fluent in a dialect that sounded like broken pieces of words and lacked every part of speech, and this morning she's an echo chamber. She thinks the garbage disposal is her pet rabbit, and unless the water is running, her lights go out. Does this constitute an emergency? Does being short-circuited and kamikaze-like meet the strict psychiatric criteria for screaming "Help" and demanding an ambulance?

I tell Crabby that we need to see Dr. Blitzer the minute he gets in. Then I walk Lola to her bedroom and ask her to get dressed.

Fifteen minutes later, I go back to check on her, and from the hallway, I see her sitting on the edge of her bed, naked from the waist up, Rubenesque, putting on a pair of panty hose. So far, so good. But drawing closer, I see she's already wearing panty hose, even though she's not wearing anything else. In fact, she's wearing half a dozen pairs, and the one she's squeezing into now will be number seven or eight. The elastic waistbands strangle her midriff like Betty Boop's. Which seems funny for a second—just a second—and then it doesn't.

I sit on the floor at my mother's feet and peel her in silence like an ear of corn, shucking the tight panty hose from the thick cob of her. Once I get her started, she continues on her own. Then momentum keeps her going even after the last pair is off. Putting her thumbs under an imaginary waistband, she slides her hands down her naked legs, and when she reaches her ankles, she lifts one foot at a time to remove an invisible pair.

Is this what *shock* turns into when it's treated with cocktails for a week?

Gradually, it dawns on me that *shock* is wrong, that *kaput* is more like it—the broken word bits, the humming, the echo, the *grrrr*-ing.

Grabbing her hands and holding them still, I try (and fail) to catch Lola's eye, wondering where she has gone and who is currently in residence in her head. Who keeps calling for more panty hose? Who thinks garbage grinders are Wonderland? Who turned up the reverb?

We've slipped into a horror movie—*Invasion of the Body Snatchers*. She's the doomed heroine who closed her eyes for a split second after a couple of drinks, and faster than you can say "happy hour," the aliens snatched her body.

And I helped. I was the assistant bartender.

I hand my naked mother her clothes one piece at a time—underpants, a bra, a blouse—in the order in which they are to be applied. I walk her to a mirror and brush her hair and hand her a tube of lipstick. But in the three seconds my back is turned, she smudges it around and around her face like Clarabell before I confiscate it and clean her up.

We get downtown much too early for her appointment, and the only thing that's open is a drive-through car wash—the first serendipity of the day, a water park. For Lola, it's Disneyland. When the waterfall begins and the soap bubbles bounce off the windshield, she starts grinning again, blushing, as though her heart is pounding joy directly to her cheeks. Or maybe, in the humidity, after all the fresh air, it's the rosy half-life of carbon monoxide seeping through her pores. How would I know?

Near the end, when we're going through the huge industrial dryer, she begins chanting something, words I can't quite hear because of the din. But at least she's talking on her own again, which is better than the echo chamber—unless it's jabberwocky.

When I pull out of the car wash, I recognize the sound of Lola's familiar English.

"Blow me blow me blow me . . ."

EIGHT

Play the Hand You're Dealt

Dr. Blitzer is a sleepy-eyed middle-aged man with a comb-over. Leaning back in his bloated leather chair behind his heavy wooden desk, he swivels between me and my mother, who hasn't said a word or even hummed since we left the car wash. The blush is off her rose, and she's withering in the witness chair. By default, I chronicle the highlights of the last twenty-four hours, confessing my role during happy hour and then telling the story in reverse, beginning with "blow me blow me" in the car wash—wondering, but not asking, whether "blow me" was Lola channeling *Bill*.

So far, Blitzer has no comment.

I act out her panty hose obsession and her garbage disposal fixation and wrap up with her word salad at the club, which was, I believe, the exact moment when Lola was snatched by the aliens. I don't tell Blitzer about the aliens—obviously.

When I get to the details of her jabberwocky, doing my best

to enunciate consonants without vowels, Blitzer clears his throat. The oracle is warming up.

"Neologism."

"That's your diagnosis?"

"No, it's a symptom. It's the technical term for what you keep calling 'jabberwocky.' "

Just what I need, a better vocabulary.

"How are you feeling, Lola?" he asks.

She doesn't answer.

"Do you know where you are?"

"Where you are where you are?" she says.

"Where are *you*, Lola?"

"Hospital."

We're actually in Blitzer's office, but that's a technicality.

"What are you doing here?"

"Having a baby."

I must have gasped, because Blitzer's glance says, Shut up or leave.

"Why are you here?"

"I'm Lithuanian."

"What year is it?"

"1917."

"How old are you?"

"How old?"

"How old are you?"

"Fifteen."

"Do you have any children?"

Turning toward me, she asks, after a beat, "Do I have any children?"

Blitzer sends me out to the waiting room.

Shortly thereafter, drawing upon his vast experience and erudition, Blitzer informs me that Lola has yet to come to terms with

Mort's death and, furthermore, is disoriented. And by the way, he "can't rule out" a nervous breakdown. This is an example of why he gets the big bucks.

He scribbles a prescription for a sedative, which I would sorely like to share—there being some logic to having the caretaker be a taster, too—but he doesn't offer. In fact, he never asks me how I am. He rips the prescription off the pad with a flourish, tendering it like a spiritual offering, and then thumbs through his appointment book. He can squeeze Lola in again for an hour at the end of the week, about three days away. Forgive me for hoping he'd take a more active interest in this psychodrama and assign my role to a night nurse. But he sends us on our way, equipped with a sedative and his illuminating diagnosis—just the usual, nothing unexpected, not for her. Which in a way is a relief.

But still, I'm the one living with her—her reluctant sidekick—and I have my doubts. Despite my long acquaintance with the borderline and the deviant, my mother has been dealt a whole new hand, and I have no idea what will turn out to be wild.

In spite of the sedative, which we don't share, and exhaustion, which we do, Lola spends a second sleepless night in the claustrophobic hallway outside our bedrooms. In a white nightgown (did I mention it was sheer?), she looks like a wraith. Her legs are rigid and her arms are aloft at her sides. She takes tiny steps, slowly and mechanically, like a spastic tightrope walker on an invisible high wire. Before each step, she lifts her knee high in the air and pauses, and then she throws her head back and pauses; and when her leg and her head come back down at the same time, she looks like she's going to topple over. Then she pauses and does it again. Not a word is spoken. Pussy circles behind her.

I switch the light on and off to snap her out of it—to reset her—but the strobe effect makes her look even creepier. *Night of the Living Dead*.

I get her a bathrobe—a peignoir, actually—and propose coffee, my usual placebo (and the only weapon other than lithium and sedatives in my armament). We chug into the kitchen, coupled like engine and caboose.

"Sit down, Mom."

"D-d-down?"

"Sit down *here*, Mom." I say it more forcefully the second time, like a flight attendant telling everyone to buckle up in bad weather.

"H-h-here?" she says, motionless.

Does stammering and being motionless mean that the sedative is kicking in?

I yank the chair out so hard, its wrought-iron legs chip the floor; the metal stutters across the tile like Lola's consonants. But Lola doesn't seem to notice. So I give her a gentle pat on the shoulder, which activates her like a windup toy with a bit of action left in its spring, and her jerky body ratchets itself down into the chair a notch at a time.

"D-d-down?" she says. "H-h-here?"

Long before the sun rises, "Taps" is playing in my head. Fluorescent light bounces off the giddy Marimekko wallpaper, and the refrigerator drones on as though everything is routine, but all the angst in the cosmos is congealing on my sticky skin. There's no ominous thunder, no black raven. The mayhem is invisible, internal. The big bang has ground to a halt, and everything is being sucked back in without a trace. Even my own compass has been smashed. Lola's fallen into a black hole where something deep and chaotic is at work, as though there's a run in the very fabric of things.

. . .

Thirty-some years ago, when Lola was in her mid-twenties, a man who looked like Abe Lincoln came to our house every Friday afternoon wearing a long black overcoat and carrying an old textbook in a leather satchel. Helen had just been born, and Ben was back in the hospital having his thumb "fixed" for the third or fourth time. In those days, Lola rarely got out of bed, because, Mort explained, she had "a back problem." Probably from too much pressure. Abe, I was told, was a masseur.

How many lies were buried in that old story?

I overheard Abe tell Nana that Lola had a neurological condition, which he called "spinal irritation." I've since learned it was an archaic diagnosis that fell out of use in the nineteenth century, although apparently no one had told that to Abe. The symptoms included "multiple tender spots distributed over the female body," and it was thought to be caused by "sexual excess." It's not hard to imagine she had the symptoms. The recommended treatment, which was "remarkably efficacious" a hundred years ago, was to apply leeches to the inside of the nostrils, and I suppose that having worms stuck up your nose would knock the sex drive out of anybody, even Lola.

I sneaked into her bedroom only once during that period, when she was in the eye of the spinal storm—not yet down for the count, but definitely horizontal. Her night table had been cleared of books and filled with a phalanx of pill bottles, three wide and two deep—maybe Abe was drugging her so she'd hold still for the leeches. He'd just left the room, and it was dark as a cave but still musky and alive. In the middle of a sunny afternoon, the shades were drawn, masking everything but two shafts of light at the window's edges. Lola was in bed, under the covers, breathing fitfully, having a nightmare, smoldering. I ran for the door and didn't return for months, convinced she was contagious.

Since then, I've learned that she was suffering, and not for the first time, from postpartum psychosis, and it isn't contagious, although it does run in families. Maybe Lola was doomed from floating around in Flossie's nasty amniotic stew. Or maybe she was doomed later, when she had the three of us and made hormonal brews of her own. "Postpartum" is why Aunt Mora and Aunt Anna decided not to have children, and it has always seemed like a sufficient reason for my genes to stop with me.

"It was nothing," Lola told me years later when I asked her about Abe. "I had a little funk, that's all. But I was allergic to the Valium that idiot doctor gave me."

At the time, before the rain hat came into vogue, there wasn't much treatment other than tranquilizers for what Lola had, and, anyway, the "idiot doctor" was just one player in a long conspiracy of underdiagnosis.

Dyspepsia, dysphoria, disinformation.

Who knows what the truth is? We are not reliable witnesses, especially of our own lives, and plenty of my own memories went down the ostrich hole. On top of the hole is a steel door with a combination lock. If there is a combination, I have lost the sequence. Maybe Lola knows it, or knew it once, but that's ancient medical history.

I pick at the twigs in the nest of my memory, but the evidence is fragile. I have occasional flashes so powerful, they happen in the present tense. But they are unconnected bright dots surrounded by darkness and mystery, like the night sky. A few images explode like shrapnel, and as the scabs get scratched, some heal and others scar, but all of them mutate. A memory of a memory is only a pale copy, and there's no way to compare it to an original. Maybe it's distorted; maybe it's airbrushed. There's no way to know. And yet, it's the map of the mind, and so a memory can never be false. If we're wrong about our memories, then what's the meaning of true and false?

In Lola's memory, the "little funk" that necessitated the Valium got worse when she took it—and then even worse when she was taken off it. And I don't know if anything relieved the "multiple tender spots" all over her body. But I suppose if anyone could have a paradoxical reaction to a tranquilizer—could get higher and crazier from a sedative—then it would be Lola.

Adverse reactions to Valium include restlessness, insomnia, and agitation. (Check.) Also nightmares and hallucinations. (Check, check.) And in severe cases, there have been instances of "derealization" and "depersonalization"—whereby both the outside world and the inner self feel unreal—and the patient requires hospitalization. (Check, check, check.)

Lo, these many years later, Abe Lincoln has expired, but now Blitzer is the bat in Lola's belfry. So Ben gets my call before dawn.

"Has she been drinking again?" is his first question. He'd already scolded me for being her enabler at happy hour the night before.

But on this night, we are both innocent.

"Is she on any new meds?"

When I read the name Navane from the pills Blitzer prescribed, Ben drops his medical mask and gasps. Blitzer, with his infuriating diagnosis of mania, has given Lola a potent central nervous system depressant that's contraindicated after coma—not unlike the mai tais I gave her, but worse. Navane, Ben tells me, is a heavy-duty antipsychotic drug that does to the central nervous system what a drag anchor does to a hot-air balloon.

"It's like tying what's left of her brain to ballast and throwing it over a cliff."

I'm standing under that cliff, wondering if there's any way I can catch my mother's brain when it falls.

I've failed as her caretaker, heaping disaster upon catastrophe, unwittingly serving her two more rounds of brain venom—

first the cocktails at the country club and then Blitzer's toxic Kool-Aid. Two poison chasers on top of Mort's poison aperitif.

What are the odds of that?

The result of this noxious recipe sits before me at the kitchen table. Rigid, bug-eyed, spastic, static, silenced. And wearing a zombie mask.

How long until *this* goes away?

"Play the hand you're dealt," Nana used to say, grounding us in her moral bedrock, the rules of poker. "Count. Don't try to beat the odds. And no bluffing."

Although her first two principles were sacrosanct, the "no bluffing" rule was never observed in our home. I faked a good hand so I could stay in the game and bet, whereas she faked a bad one so the pot would get bigger. Drawing a card, she'd bite her lower lip and grimace, then pull a pencil out of her bun and pretend to calculate something. I should have known she didn't need paper to count cards, and besides, she was a terrible actress. But my desire to believe her—and the hope that I could win one—outweighed her weak performance.

"This time you really got my tit caught in a wringer," she'd say.

Hell, if her hand is bad, mine must be fabulous, I'd think. So I'd see her last bet and Helen would raise and Ben would double, and the minute she knew she had us, she'd flash a full house and wipe all our chips into her gargantuan pile.

Then the lessons began: "Ya gotta know when to fold."

She dedicated herself to enriching our vocabularies and training the sucker out of us, but folding is something not one of us ever mastered. Even now, I keep drawing cards until there are no more coming.

. . .

After reading Blitzer the riot act, Ben makes Lola an appointment for later in the day—putting her in a temporary holding pattern until he can figure out where to land her case. Meanwhile, since Navane is such an effective antidote to both speech and movement (particularly among those who've recently endured traumatic brain injuries), Lola's primary activity is mumbling.

I need air. But before taking a quick jog, I lay Lola's clothes out beside her on her bed, where she's been resting for hours in her wraithlike peignoir. *The worst that could happen*, if I'm gone for half an hour, is she'll wrap herself up in a dozen pairs of panty hose. No one ever died of a strangled waist.

But a mile away, along Reservoir Avenue, with the dappled June sunlight wrapping the dewy rosebuds in promise, with oxygen flowing freely through my sleep-deprived brain for the first time in days, it suddenly hits me that the sedative could wear off at any instant, and Lola could right this very second be testing the blades of the garbage disposal.

I am galvanized.

My lazy legs leap into action and I, who rarely lift my heels from the pavement, sprint home like Mercury, *preparing for the worst*. I'll grab a dishrag as a tourniquet for her fingers and scoop her sliced knuckles and shredded cartilage from the drain and pack them in a Tupperware container with ice from the ice maker, if it's working, and race her and the container to a hospital for a microsurgery reunion. Will my smart thinking after her mauling compensate for the negligence that caused it?

I may represent Disaster, but I am also Rescue.

Racing through the front door, gasping, guilt-ridden, penitent, pathetic, I listen for her screaming but hear nothing. Just the air conditioner kicking in. What a relief.

Unless she's already bled to death.

I run into her room and find her where I left her, on the bed, like an android on standby, although now she's sitting up. And she's naked.

Her white nightgown has been discarded, and her clothes, even the panty hose, lie untouched. A permanently uninhabited look has settled on her face.

"This is different," I tell Blitzer. "This isn't Aunt Flossie taking over her thinking. She's not wild; she's anaesthetized."

"No affect," he says with no affect.

"It's like she's on empty."

"Catatonia."

"She's not catatonic; she moves—but like she's on a high wire, lifting her knees up and throwing her head back."

"Equine gait." He straightens up in his big chair.

"She stammers like a stuck needle."

"Perseveration."

"And she parrots back what I say."

"Echolalia." He writes it down.

Annoying amounts of time elapse while he mulls things over, tapping his thumbs together as though they'll generate a spark of thought, his head bobbing like a doll's on a dashboard.

"Your mother's thinking is profoundly disorganized," he announces, as though her brain is a messy closet. "I believe the stress of recent events has pushed her into another spell."

"A *spell?*" I repeat. Where did this guy study?

"An *episode*. An *episode* of bipolar disorder. Incidentally, your brother wants a neurologist to see her, so I'll arrange for that in the morning."

"What's wrong with *now?* She can't be left alone even for a minute."

Do I sound as alarmed as I feel? Should I grab a bullhorn and belt into his ear "WHAT ABOUT THE GARBAGE DIS-

POSAL, DOC?" Sure, I wrapped it in duct tape—but wouldn't a straitjacket be more secure?

He puts her name on the waiting list for a bed at Shady Tree Sanitarium, where she has spent many a more agitated night, but I can't understand why she isn't admitted immediately and given an upgrade.

On a nostalgic cruise through the neighborhood where we used to live, the historic East Side of Providence, I point out her friends' brick Colonials and mannered Tudors set back from well-tended lawns. I take the long way home, top down, to blow fresh air through her mental clutter and mine, although I no longer think our problems will be solved by pleasant breezes. I drive by the Pizza Palace off Hope Street, where I hung out after junior high, feeding my acne, and the East Side Diner, whose Boston cream pies became the main ingredient in my thighs.

Circling the city's most august synagogue, which was rarely blessed with my presence after the Bar Mitzvah party years, I drive verrrrry slooooowly, as though five minutes of worshipful loitering now could lift the pox on our house and make up for my lifelong truancy (read: atheism). At this moment, I'd be relieved to discover my mother hiding in the rabbi's study, composing Talmudic anagrams, bridging the distance to the golden mean, rearranging the cosmos the way most moms dust knickknacks. Instead, she's oblivious, inert, immobile, and spin-free.

The final stop on memory lane is our first house, a small two-story brick Colonial on Fifth Street, its front yard graced by a lush pink cherry tree, the one Hellish nearly decapitated twenty years ago when she landed in its branches after sliding down the drainpipe to escape from her room—while Lola stood in the vestibule, screaming at her like a banshee, and then chased her up the street. I pull over, narrating the highlights of our years there—snow so deep that she built me an igloo, the leaky skating rink Mort made out of dry-cleaner bags, the limbo contests where she went bump in the night.

None of this jump-starts her.

In the fifties, in this little brick house, I began navigating the huge divide between Lola's actual carnal antics and her staid motherly advice. My six-year-old sidekick, Ricky Goodman, lived across the street and played in my room after school—mostly Parcheesi and Monopoly—but by the time we were in first grade, I was bored by board games. I thought we should play penis and vagina. (The mezuzah doesn't fall far from the doorpost.)

I didn't tell Ricky my game plan, of course, since I knew by then that boys had to think everything was their idea. Instead, I set up a sham wrestling match and told him that the winner could do ANYTHING he wanted to the loser. So we wrestled, and I pretended to lose.

"Now you can do anything you want to me," I told Ricky, and he tickled me for ten seconds. He wasn't the swiftest boy in the neighborhood.

So we wrestled a second time and then a third, and each time after I lost, I told him he could do ANYTHING he wanted to me.

He wanted me to stand on my head. He wanted me to act like a monkey. He wanted me to get him a cookie. It was obvious that Ricky needed more direction.

And so I explained that after the next—and final—match, the winner could make the loser pull down his or her pants. And then—*woops*—I lost again.

"On the count of three," Ricky proclaimed, "you have to pull down your pants!"

"Only if you do, too," I told him.

So we shut the door to my room and stood facing each other a few feet apart on my bed, and on the count of three—"One, two, threeeeeeee"—we both pulled down our pants. Ricky's little dickie yawned in the air like a groundhog, the first time it had ever been oxygenated, while my pale, hairless vagina peeked out from its white cotton enclosure like a newborn.

But at that very instant, my bedroom door opened wide, and of course it was Lola, shrieking as though Ricky's peckless pecker were a cherry picker.

It would be many years before I pulled down my pants again, and when I finally did, I remembered to lock my door.

Meantime, my instructions from Lola the nun, who was busy sashaying around the neighborhood under her limbo stick when she wasn't lecturing me on virtue, were to keep all the boys "dangling" at a safe distance. Playing hard to get, she explained, would make them surround me "with their tongues hanging out"—an image that gave me nightmares of a long lineup of deranged droolers. To this day, I can't think about Ricky Goodman's boxers, or even his tongue, without pulling the covers over my head.

Unfortunately, even in the sixties, the hormonal drumbeat in my mind was drowned out by Lola's ersatz Catholicism. In an era famous for sex, drugs, and rock 'n' roll, I can vouch for the bands and the grass, but woefully little was actually consummated in the love department.

Other Lola-isms demanded immediate action. "It's better to be married and divorced than never to be married at all," she cautioned me when my ring finger failed to sprout a diamond in both high school and college. "Besides," she added, "you need a man to take care of you."

So while I continued my search for Mr. Right, I also continued my search for a new mother.

The guiding principle of my childhood was not to turn out like Lola, but there was a shortage of alternatives. Not for one instant did it ever occur to me to be myself.

When I was little, I thought about being Cousin Madeline, primarily because Lola and Mort regularly told me, "You're just like your cousin Madeline." But immediately after this pronouncement, they sent me to my room. Naturally, I had second thoughts about her.

Eventually, I settled on Barbara Walters. She wasn't really old enough to be my mother, but so what? There she was—live, sane, and successful—every day on *Today*, crashing through the looming ubiquitous glass ceiling. What girl didn't want to be Barbara Walters? *She* didn't seem to need anybody to take care of her; she seemed to be taking pretty good care of herself.

As a backup, in case Barbara Walters wasn't interested, I cast Barbara Parkins, especially in the last scene of *Valley of the Dolls*, where she's walking through the snowy Vermont woods in her old mink, plotting a novel, after she's turned her back on her glamorous life as a model in New York.

Once I found a mother, I wouldn't need much more, I figured.

"A man, a dog, or a book," my friend Louise Bernikow wrote, wondering, like me, if she could have all three.

Back home after our day trip down memory lane, nestled into Lola's cozy vinyl-sided apartment complex, with its Formica cabinets and faux-wood walls, I prep *boeuf à la ficelle*. Our conversation is limited to the sound of my own words boomeranging. My sous-chef separates thyme leaves from their stems (sorting is one of the last skills to go), but then she throws the leaves into the garbage can and the stems into my silky sauce.

After dinner, she marches off to her bedroom, returning when I'm engaged in her favorite activity, running the garbage disposal. She's put on two nightgowns, a green one with a boa and a frilly red number on top—both see-through. Growing up in her grandfather's triple-decker tenement, Lola used to wander up to the top floor, which was rented out to Madame Dorée—a floozy who was always dressed for bed and whose sheer negligees had a lifelong impact on Lola's choice of sleepwear. Tonight, I put her to bed wrapped up like a nylon Christmas ornament. *What difference does it make? Who's gonna see her?*

Before dawn, she wanders into my room "brushing" her teeth with a comb, scraping the plastic up and down against her gums with excellent dental technique. It's creepy, but I can actually follow her "logic." Words that sound alike *are* alike. One thing's as good as another. A brush is a brush is a comb.

Later that morning, she's admitted to Shady Tree, a sprawling redbrick campus in a wooded enclave at the end of a luxurious boulevard, less than a mile from our family's first home on Fifth Street. At Admissions, Mrs. Fleming, the head social worker, asks Lola to sign the voluntary-institutionalization form, since I have the desire but not the right to commit her.

Lola scribbles "5/5/5/5/5/5/5/5/5/5/5/5/5/5/5/5" on the page.

Mrs. Fleming's face registers confusion, and she removes the pen from Lola's hand.

See? I want to say. What is that about?

Instructing us to "wait right here," Mrs. Fleming slips away, and I take the liberty of reading Lola's chart, beginning with Dr. Blitzer's notes. "Presumptive diagnosis of bipolar disorder following death of husband—depressed, following a mildly manic episode.*" I follow the asterisk to the next page. "*Now felt to be suffering from side effects of Navane." Then, in different handwriting, is Mrs. Fleming's assessment: "Disoriented. Robotlike. Grossly unkempt. Psychotic?"

I can't quibble with the terms *disoriented* or *robotlike*—no reasonable person would—but *psychotic*, which suddenly feels blindingly obvious, hadn't occurred to me on my own. And *psy-*

chotic is the jackpot here at Shady Tree—it's "the secret word." A Groucho duck ought to drop out of the ceiling and award Mrs. Fleming a hundred-dollar bill.

The neurologist, a tall, gaunt man in a long white coat, comes into the waiting room and calls Lola's name. Which elicits no response. I point to her. *Grossly unkempt* fills me with shame. How could I have forgotten to groom her? How could I send my mother off to a perfectly respectable asylum looking insane?

The doctor comes over and introduces himself. He stands Lola up, takes her arm, and leads her away.

I watch them disappear down the corridor—the giant scientist and his small stiff subject. She's an alien robot on a high wire, hobbling from side to side, then lurching forward. He steadies her arm and coaxes her into his exam room, where I lose sight of both of them. Then I exhale.

I don't know what kind of ingredients he stocks in his formulary, but I'm counting on him to whip up a huge batch of Navane antidote, and if he feels he absolutely must, let him warm up her old rain hat.

NINE

Lola Redux

Of the many lessons learned at my mother's knee, "Make hay while the sun shines" is my all-time-favorite Lola-ism. It was a literal rule when I was a kid—get to the beach before the clouds blow in—but as I got older, I gleaned adult corollaries that extended into the wee small hours, the limbo-stick sexfest being a prime example. So the instant I am liberated from Shady Tree, I head for the beach with the top down, belting "Summer in the City" with the Lovin' Spoonful, feigning the carefree abandon of the teenager who hitchhiked these country roads in a simpler time. An hour later, in the quaint town of Barrington, I meet an old boyfriend for an afternoon at the beach, where the combination of unfinished business and sunburned glow lead to an evening in his bed.

Sex, I learned from an expert, is nature's way of giving grief the middle finger.

Jack is a brilliant, rugged historian I fell in love with in graduate school, when he was in his thirties, after he'd just left the Jesuits and was making up for lost carnal time (monogamously, with me). Every morning upon awakening, he outlined our day's sexual agenda, planning where and how he would waylay me—in his kitchen before breakfast, in front of the fireplace during lunch, on his sailboat before and after sunset—which was at first a welcome confirmation of my charms. But after a few tender months with Jack, I was chafing under his romantic expectations by brunch and trying to figure out how to make it upright through cocktails. Tonight, ten years later, long defrocked but still frisky, Jack was just the ticket.

Back at Lola's apartment after midnight, not so distracted by a romantic interlude that I forget the main narrative is a horror story, I move from the pullout couch in the den to my parents' empty double bed. I am Goldilocks. There is symbolism in this act, which I plan to review in the morning. But it's a restless night from the beginning, first because Pussy's little cat feet dance under the door, protesting his lockout, and then because of a call before dawn.

"*Hallo oui*," I say, forgetting I'm not in Paris anymore.

"Sorry to wake you, but this is Highbridge Nursing Home, and we have some bad news."

Bad news from a new source. How nice. Highbridge is where Aunt Flossie lives.

Or lived.

Without further ado, I slam her coffin shut and launch it toward the grave.

"Your aunt needs one of her toes amputated."

"Aunt Flossie is *alive?*"

This must strike the caller as flippant, because her voice turns from officious to prickly. But when "bad news" was announced, I jumped to *the worst that could happen*, so I could *prepare myself*.

"Yes, of course your aunt is still alive!" Prickly exclaims, not bothering to hide her disapproval. "Mrs. Hornstein needs to authorize the surgery."

"Not very likely." Recalling Lola's chicken scratches on the admissions form at Shady Tree, I can't imagine her grappling with surgical consent.

"Well she has to," Prickly insists, annoyed at my impertinence. "We can't operate without authorization from next of kin."

"I'll authorize it."

Given recent trends, amputation's not a bad option. Hell, just one little toe? Full speed ahead!

Prickly is skeptical, since we got off on the wrong foot. "Well, you'll have to come down here and sign the papers and prove you're responsible."

"How can I prove I'm *responsible?*" I hear myself ask. The notion is preposterous.

"Bring your driver's license. I'll be waiting."

"*Now?* It's the middle of the night."

"Now would be fine. We'll amputate first thing in the morning."

Prickly is satisfied.

Take the damn toe. What the hell, while she's under, help yourself to a few of them. It's Aunt Flossie's turn to offer a small sacrifice.

Then we'll see who's next.

Back at Shady Tree by lunchtime, I find that the floor nurse wants to catch me up on what she's learned from her first night with Lola. She looks exhausted.

"Your mother is unredirectable," she begins, putting a fresh spin on the body snatching. "She's disoriented, her speech is garbled, and she repeats the same phrases ad nauseam. I had to help her with the simplest tasks—brushing her teeth, dressing. And she wanders. I couldn't leave her alone for a minute."

Old news. This is where I came in.

But it's not the end of her story.

After dinner, she tells me, Lola stripped down to her bra and panties and "moseyed," through the room next door. The nurse doesn't define "moseyed," and I don't ask. And she doesn't need to tell me it was a man's room.

"The orderlies had to bring her back and put her in restraints. And not long after that, she wet her bed."

Why would my mother wet her bed?

I find her in a small private room, staring out the window, her back to me. She's in a wheelchair, wearing a seat belt. Her fingers twirl in the air like ballerinas and she's mumbling something—numbers, I think.

Pointing to the wheelchair, the nurse says, too gently, "Your mom is having some trouble walking, dear."

Understating the disaster.

My mother turns toward me—and she's still wearing the zombie mask.

"Mrs. Hornstein, look. Your daughter is here."

"Daughter is here daughter is here . . ." Lola leans around me because I'm blocking her view of the door—where her daughter must be.

"I'm right *here*." I tap her shoulder, since my face is insufficient to identify me.

"Right here right here right here . . ."

Maybe I need more evidence. I pull out an old photo I brought from her night table—of her at twenty, grinning in front of a sun-drenched clothesline, where pink baby towels and white diapers are drying. She's holding a wicker laundry basket with a baby in it: me.

She puts the photo in her lap and looks at me curiously. Then her hands go back to their pas de deux.

The moments pass in silent, sweaty jump cuts: The nurse holds up a clean bedpan—she smiles—she leaves—she shuts the door—Lola finishes *Swan Lake*—she fidgets with her fingernails—I straighten her glasses—she plays an invisible piano, humming along in Lithuanian—I straighten her glasses again and again, until I realize they won't stay straight because it's her face that's lopsided—one eyebrow is arched, the other not, as though only half of her is here, or both halves are here but are currently incommunicado.

The nurse comes back with a tray. "Your daughter will feed you." She smiles.

"That's nice that's nice," Lola says, sideswiping the tray, making the fork ricochet off her wheelchair and clatter onto the floor. Regardless, her empty hand shuttles back and forth between the plate and her mouth, which keeps opening and closing, empty but expectant. She does this over and over again, despite getting no result. She's oblivious to being strapped to a wheelchair in a claustrophobic room, to being spastic and incoherent and amnesiac. But she knows she's hungry.

Grabbing a spoon, I feed her meat loaf and mashed potatoes. "That's nice," she says, the only words she originates. And when I feed her rice pudding, her favorite, she says "very nice"—adding the word *very* but not the inflection that generally accompanies it.

Nothing varies her monotone. Her speech is a shell now, brittle and cracked. And the Navane has turned her inside out. So despite her incoherence, I can see through her zombie mask, all the way inside my mother—to her core, where I thought the cherry was buried.

My whole family used to be terrorized by what Lola held inside. Her variegated therapies—the sleep therapy, the drug therapy, the shock therapy—they were all in service of a single goal: Don't let what's inside her get out. Push it down. Bury it. Seal it up. Talk therapy might let it out, so give her shock therapy to wipe it out. If it starts to surface, notify the authorities. If she brings up Aunt Flossie or Bill, plug her directly into the rain hat.

Still, the deeper I tried to bury that cherry, the more power it had over me.

Now, for the first time, I can see beyond it, inside the secret spot where I thought all her darkness congealed: *Here lies the center of the universe*. Maybe it never was the black hole I imagined. But if it was, the center has not held. She's a wisp of smoke that was snuffed out while I was tending her embers, still afraid of the spark that was always too hot to touch.

I haven't touched my mother for twenty years. Sure, I permit her cheek to graze mine on birthdays, and I make a perfunctory gesture when I come and go. But I always try to have luggage in my hand so that no hugging is necessary, because I never doubted until this moment that she was contagious.

Underneath all her fiery madness, it turns out, there's no monster after all, only a gentle, uncritical soul whose simple-hearted sweetness is summed up by her simple-minded mantra, "That's nice."

After years of cringing when she put her cheek near mine, of treating her like a virus I might catch—as though I was the victim, not she—this seems like a good time to pull her close to me.

I drag a bench over to her wheelchair, and although I am awkward, although the metal wheel is digging into my rib cage and she's playing the air piano, I slip my arms around my mother's neck and bury my nose in her hair.

Does she know me now? Does she feel me banging on the window to her soul, now that it's slammed shut?

A sitcom laugh track drifts in from another room until she nods off.

Her head slips onto my shoulder.

I look at her and at myself hugging her.

And after a while, she begins to drool.

At the end of her first week at Shady Tree—a month after the boat accident, when Lola has no more lucid moments, when the gibberish is nonstop, when "she requires supervision for all activities except eating," which she does with both hands, when the wheelchair is her permanent seat assignment and she can no longer ask to get up—after breakfast on day seven, she defecates in bed.

Her neurologist, Dr. Greely, calls me personally to deliver the news. "I wish I could offer you some encouragement" is what he says, right after "Hello."

Doctors with bad news never waste time. And why should they? They know.

"Another nervous breakdown," I say, *preparing myself* for the inevitable.

"You could put it that way," he says, "but her condition isn't *psych*ological—it's *neur*ological."

At last I'm talking to an expert—although I'm not immediately sure whether neurological is better or worse than my own diagnosis. It sounds deeper and maybe more sinister.

And it is.

Lola is suffering from a delayed consequence of what he calls "the original insult," carbon-monoxide toxicity—which is when he started counting (I've been counting since her first shock treatment). And the toxic reaction was "fueled," he says, by Navane, which is "the secondary insult" (not counting the mai tais). The Navane's effect is temporary (he believes), but right now it's exacerbating the underlying problem. Once it's completely out of her system, he'll get a better sense of "the *real damage*." He doesn't explain what "real damage" means. (And I don't ask.) Nevertheless, he continues, he's sure the "myelin" around her nerves has deteriorated, and that it's still deteriorating. He's also certain that her "neural highway has been interrupted." He repeats that. He's very sure about the detour on her highway.

What a *fantasy echo* this is turning out to be. Lola's brain was in a highway accident. Myelin is where the rubber meets the road. Currently there are potholes in her *myelin*, and things will get worse before they get better. I have no trouble imagining the rest of it, beginning with the road repair—he'll reinflate her like a blown tire so she can get off this old highway and make a U-turn. Then he'll repave her with the cerebral equivalent of asphalt. Fine. At least she's in capable hands.

How long until she gets better? That's all I want to know.

But it seems that I've missed his point: We haven't seen the worst of it yet. That's what he's trying to tell me. As though he has a crystal ball.

This is not like a "detour," he says, correcting my analogy but running with it. This is more like a "dead end." He apologizes for his bad pun, then illustrates why it's so well chosen, running through "the highlights of the delayed onset of encephalopathy." Pretty much everything that makes us human disappears: memory, thought, speech, motion, emotion. And, of course, inhibition. Also toilet training. Which brings the conversation full circle, to the incident that initiated it, the bed soiling. And within a week or two, he predicts, we'll see the rest of it.

"Things heal. Bones knit," I sputter. Lola always bounces back.

"What's done is done," he says sagely. "Brain tissue does not regenerate."

Then he repeats two words like a chant, like I'll get it if he says them enough times: *permanent* and *irreversible*, *permanent* and *irreversible*, *permanent* and *irreversible*, until they sound like one word, *permversable*, *permversable*, *permversable*.

He tells me if I saw her MRI, I'd understand. "It looks like someone used Wite-Out on her gray matter." And it's only going to get worse. Just ahead, *so prepare yourself*, is a big, bottomless neural sinkhole—the fissure at the center of the universe.

Shouldn't we get a second opinion?

"Don't kid yourself," Greely says. There's nothing Shady Tree can do for Lola—she probably can't be helped anywhere else, either—but it's time to move her to a different type of institution. One that's equipped to deal with *permversability*.

He reels off the phone number of the hospital social worker and says she'll explain the details. He wishes he could offer me some encouragement, but he can't.

"Hope would be counterproductive," he tells me, like he's Dr. Kevorkian.

And he's sorry. But myelin is where the rubber meets the road.

I realize I'm supposed to be brave, since false calm counts as dignity during tragedy. I hear myself say "Thank you." And then I hang up and sit at the kitchen table, crying over the hand that's just been dealt.

The kitchen is filled with snapshots of a life that's been canceled: Mort and Lola holding hands in the Uffizi Gallery; kissing on a boat in the "floating gardens" of Mexico; swimming in Lake George; the two of them taking the three of us to Story Land, where she told more tales than Mother Goose.

Her bulletin board overflows with alphabetical shopping lists (brisket, cat food, chicken wings, dental floss) and invitations to parties, canasta games, golf tournaments, and charity meetings. This week, she was scheduled to address the Paraplegic Association, which she founded after a friend's accident. Instead, it looks like she'll amortize her contribution.

I stare at the social worker's phone number, my mind paralyzed but racing. Which is to say that my thoughts are speeding even though they're stuck in place. Around and around they whir, wheels stuck in a rut without traction, burning rubber.

Is that what Lola's thoughts are like now?

It's trouble, a poet said, when a sapling bends in a stiff wind. But it's tragedy when the tree breaks.

Growing up in the eye of Lola's storm, her three little saplings got blown about and twisted plenty. The trouble drove us away from her, but it also drove us forward—and it held us together—which may be why we didn't break.

Only Lola got broken.

When we were kids, Ben and I usually studied in our rooms after dinner, and Helen, who was "the wild child," hid behind the dining room curtains while the adults sat around drinking coffee, talking in hushed voices about Lola's treatments. Nana never understood why any of it was necessary, since she'd watched most of her family get sucked into the undertow, and no doctors ever made anyone better for long.

"Won't Lola get electrocuted?" she asked my father.

"It's electric *therapy*, Leah, not electro*cution*," he explained, wearily, for the third or fourth time. "They don't turn it up that high."

Helen ran upstairs to tell us. "Mommy's getting electric-fried."

"Not *fried*," Ben said, correcting her. "*Fide*. F-I-D-E. She's getting electri-*fide*." He already had a natural air of medical authority.

"So how do they do it?" she asked him.

"They just plug her in," he reassured her.

"Like a lamp? She'll light up?"

He thought it over. "No, not like a lamp. Like the Mixmaster."

I had no idea what he was talking about, and even Helen knew he was making it up. "Nana says the doctors are gonna stupid-fy Mommy."

"Mommy will never be stupid," he said.

And that was true. Lola's doctors threw the therapeutic book at her for years, but none of their treatments stupid-fied her, not permanently anyway. That distinction belongs to the *Mr. Fix It* and the Navane chaser. Apparently, they've stupid-fied her for good.

I'd been convinced she was going to come out of it, that this "spell" would lift, like the others, like darkness. She was better, brighter, early on, but that was before the cerebral sequelae caught up with her.

The light I saw in her then was the trail of her comet, and the glow she gave off had already been snuffed out—like a dead star falling through the night sky: By the time it's visible overhead, it's already passed by. I could have aerated her every second we were together, but it wouldn't have made a difference: Cerebral sequelae will not be denied.

"She has a hell of a lot of nerve," people used to say.

Well, maybe she did. But it's all gone now.

TEN

Curiosity

Pussy the cat has managed to stay in the background, content to be part of the context without usurping the plot. He's tolerating his bedroom lockout and new diet, eating every desiccated scientific pellet I drop in his bowl to replace the leftovers Lola served—fish cakes and clam's casino—and using the litter box faithfully, not my shoe or pillow. Yet just when I assume he's thriving, he fails to appear for breakfast, and there's plaintive meowing coming from the living room.

Lying on the floor, flat as a fur rug, his front paws swim in my direction, but the back legs are deadweight. I give him a once-over, unable to find blood or broken bones, but a lamp cord seems to run through him on the way to a wall socket. A closer inspection reveals teeth marks on the wire. Which explains the smell of burned hair, or burned whiskers, or maybe both. Even a confirmed skeptic would have to allow that this household is a magnet for disaster.

Wrapping him in a blanket, I make a dash for the vet, whose waiting room is overflowing, but our case rises right to the top. One thing you can say for disaster: You get very good service.

Pussy is carted off to a back room, where a medical team works on him for an hour while I read old *People* magazines, and eventually a sweaty ectomorph, Dr. Denial himself, comes into the waiting room, bowing deferentially and whispering in the obsequious tones generally reserved for a funeral parlor. "You can see him now."

"He's *alive?*" (I hear myself ask this frequently.) He rushes me down a corridor but doesn't answer my question. Which, I know, is a hint.

In a surgical suite that reeks of rubbing alcohol, there's enough high-tech equipment to rival Lola's room in intensive care, and Pussy's hooked up to all of it. A cardiac monitor with long leads terminates in two little bald spots on his chest. Mounted on a stainless-steel table, he is testimony to the power of medical technology to restore the dead to an indefinable state that's short of life.

"Is he in a coma?"

"Not exactly. We were able to bring him around."

I *prepare myself* for the "however."

"However, he won't be quite himself."

"Meaning what?" The possibilities are endless.

"He won't be able to do all the things he once did."

"He never actually did very much." Pussy's only trick was hiding under the bed and snagging Lola's panty hose. Given her current fixation, he's got his work cut out for him.

"Is he alive?" I ask a second time.

At well over six feet, the vet, who's been hovering over me like a helicopter, swoops down precipitously, as though I'm a dwarf, and he peers into my eyes—consolingly.

"We thought we'd lost him a couple of times, but . . ." Pointing to the defibrillator, he twinkles with pride.

In my opinion, the resurrection is unconvincing, although in his current state, Pussy would be the perfect pet for Lola.

A prickly drop of sweat tickles the back of my neck. Fight or flight, my body says, and it is flight I choose. It takes all my energy to pull myself out of the vet's force field, so wide is the net of anxiety he's cast around me, but I yank myself from the room, away from his impending prognosis, and beat it down the hall.

He comes after me, shouting, "The problem is that we're not sure how long he went without oxygen."

I knew it.

"And what does that mean?" As if I don't already know. It means *permversable* brain damage.

"We'll monitor him for a few days and then conduct some more tests."

"More tests? For days?"

Look at this equipment! We don't have pet insurance and the coins are tumbling into the vet slot machine. *K-ching, k-ching*.

How do you calculate a respectable amount of time to keep a cat alive? Is two hours enough? Two days? When is hope legitimately exhausted? And why would I willingly add this beast to my burdens?

Why? Because the sign in my head reads DO THE RIGHT THING. Keeping the cat alive would certainly please Lola, who has no use for money that isn't being spent and who might, conceivably, come out of her own oxygen deprivation screaming for her kitty.

Suppose her first words are *Where's my Pussy?* The possibilities for guilt are endless. *How long did you wait before you murdered my cat?* How could I tell her that I was too cheap to wait twenty-four hours for Pussy to come around and had him gassed on day one? And how tasteless would gassing be after her own ordeal? And wouldn't that make everyone suspect that I'd had the same impulse when it came to Lola herself, that I'd sniffed around the intoxicating edges of euthanasia for *all* the members of her household?

"This must be very hard for you," the vet says.

What's hard is cutting my losses, folding with a rotten hand when the dealer is pretending there are still cards to be drawn. Could I figure out which plug to pull? Or would I yank the urine drip instead of the lung machine and be ankle-deep in cat piss when the alarms go off? Should I leave Franken-Pussy here with an open tab on my American Express card? Or take him back to Paris with me when he's well enough to fly coach?

I'd like to beg the vet to put a DO NOT RESUSCITATE sign over his stainless-steel shelf, which is, I recognize, the same instinct I have for Aunt Flossie. But Dr. Denial is looking at me with such tender pity, and he's just spent an hour restoring his patient to something resembling taxidermy. So how can I ask him to put me out of the misery of my mother's cat?

"It's not my cat. It's my mother's."

"This will be a terrible shock to her."

"I doubt it. Nothing could shock her now."

ELEVEN

The Thing with Feathers

Ben and Helen fly in the next day, right after they hear Dr. Greely's prognosis. I don't mention the Pussy problem until they arrive. But I'd chosen not to sit by Pussy's bedside with my fingers on his little cat temples, and during the night, he went on his own to his final reward.

Thank god I didn't have to pull the plug.

May he find an afterlife of unrun panty hose. And may his claws be eternally sharp. Amen.

When we arrive at Shady Tree, Lola is in adult Pampers and quilted sweatpants, stuffed like a pear into the peanut-size seat of a wheelchair. She's wearing her zombie mask, which I now know is *permversable*.

Although she seems to respond appropriately when we walk into her room, she can't recall our names or put two coherent thoughts together, so preoccupied is she with counting in her new math—after "ten" comes "ten-dy-one, ten-dy-two, ten-dythree." And when she's not counting, she's talking to herself nonstop, although she doesn't seem to understand a thing she says.

Dr. Greely has diagnosed "fluent aphasia"—he explains that our words, and even her own words, might as well be Greek to her. She can't comprehend any of it, and that's why she talks nonsense.

"How do you feel, Mom?"

"Get the tickets."

"What tickets?"

"That's nice."

"Look, we brought you flowers."

"A word to the wise."

Lola is a one-woman solipsistic party in her personal Tower of Babel. And according to Greely, it's all downhill from here.

Helen is silent, ashen. I'd told her, but apparently she didn't *prepare herself*. Such is the difference between hearsay and firsthand experience.

Among the battery of tests Lola has recently endured, her IQ has been pegged at twenty-nine. Did she really need to take an IQ test to demonstrate she's in no condition for puzzles and word games? My mother, who beat adults at card games from the time she was three, who replicated the periodic table after giving it a passing glance, no longer knows her name, her location, or the date. The keen tester, who'd never met her before but was told her three children all hold advanced degrees, put himself out on a ledge and surmised she's had a "precipitous decline." I'm guessing it's an 80 percent markdown. I never actually knew my mother's IQ before the accident, but when I was growing up, its near infinitude was family folklore, a number so high that you dared not ask, lest your own meager helping be put into relief.

I watch Helen try to snap into therapist mode, conducting a test I don't follow—her version, I guess, of Ben's Babinski. She gives Lola a pen and paper and tells her to write her name. Lola draws a circle within a circle within a circle—the same way she put on her lipstick—and that must be the wrong answer, because Helen starts to cry.

Ben takes Lola's hands in his, pressing them to his face to catch her eye, to look through the vacant window to her soul.

She purses her lips to form a word as he leans in.

"Eleven-dy-one."

When he encourages her, she continues.

"Eleven-dy-two."

Then she stops.

There was a time when my mother could repeat dozens of numbers and often did so to amuse us. She calculated the square roots of the license plates on the cars in front of us. She memorized pi to thirty decimals and would happily recite the numbers backward to pass time in traffic. Numbers were how she concentrated. Now, "eleven-dy-two" is as good as it gets. I know this because Greely has a crystal ball.

We may not have had the double funeral Ben prepared me for, but the second coffin is slipping into mental quicksand, even though the woman inside is still alive.

Ben wheels Lola out, past the nurses' station, where all heads are lowered, although no one seems particularly busy. But I don't blame them—grief is an airborne contaminant and no one is immune.

What exactly did Kierkegaard say was "the sickness unto death"—the specific emotional state that marks the end of happiness? Was it pessimism? Despair? Dread?

I say it's the moment when hope becomes counterproductive. I say it's *permversability*.

Outside in the sun, it is a glorious, glistening, otherwise normal day at the end of June. The world has been going on, as it tends to do, and the cool spring that killed our father has turned into a warm summer. Roses perfume the winding path we take, and Ben parks Lola in the shade of an old maple tree.

Her hands do a cat's cradle without string.

She plays air harp.

And she counts. "Twelve-dy-one . . . twelve-dy-two . . ." She counts on and on. And when she gets to eighteen, she stops.

Helen smiles. "She made it to eighteen."

Ben nods.

Then they hug each other.

"She counted her way to *chai*," Helen says.

I am the last to get it, as usual. Just when everything looks random to me, my siblings uncover a pattern. *Chai* means "life" in Hebrew; and in numerology, the letters add up to eighteen. Lola always sent us checks for eighteen dollars on our birthdays and Jewish holidays. Eighteen is her magic number.

So it appears that despite the dead ends on her neurological highway, our mother is still practicing a feebleminded form of Gamatria and is trying to count her way back to *life*.

The realization that she's aware of her sorry state and fighting it gives my siblings hope—but it has the opposite effect on me. For me, this is the sickness unto death. I thought Lola had already given up the struggle and slipped peacefully beneath the undertow, that she was going down, but at least she was going down in peace. I figured "the limits of her language were the limits of her world." That was what Wittgenstein said.

"What can be said at all can be said clearly," he wrote. "All we know is what we have words for."

That made sense to me; it *relieved* me, in some strange way. And whenever I read something into one of her remarks, I beat myself back with a cognitive stick. But now I find out that this woman for whom "hope would be counterproductive" is nonetheless aware enough of her condition to be doing brain-damaged kabbalah.

"Eighteen," Ben repeats, kneeling in front of her, the gravel pitting his knees. "Eighteen."

"Dr. Greely says there's no hope," I whisper.

"*He* has no hope," Ben shoots back.

"So he's wrong?" I never question medical authority—I just try to figure out who has more of it.

"How should I know? No one can know. No one can *make* you give up hope."

No? I'd say *the thing with feathers* has clipped wings.

"Eighteen," Ben says again. My brother is going to be the last to fold.

When the sun falls behind the trees and our little vale gets chilly, we find a music room with an old upright piano, and Ben rolls Lola up to the keyboard beside him. We all know the funereal Chopin étude, the gloomy, romantic dirge that's become his running musical commentary, and Lola hums along while playing broken chords on her air piano.

From time to time, she farts.

"That's nice," she says.

We wheel her back to her room, and as we're leaving, she defecates in bed.

The social worker who's been assigned to the case explains that the world is divided into two kinds of nursing homes—the not-so-nice kind, for incontinent adults, and the nice kind, where everybody takes themselves to the bathroom. Lola has to go to the shitty kind permanently unless she gets toilet-trained fast. And we already know what Greely thinks her chances are.

"Changing of the guard," Helen tells me, handing me the flight schedule to Paris. And this certainly looks more like her slice of the Lola pie than mine. Before she flew into town, Helen visited a neurologist friend and told him Lola's current diagnosis. He'd never treated "delayed cerebral sequelae of carbon-monoxide poisoning," and so they went to the medical library and researched it together. "You're in for one hell of a ride," he told her. And so Helen took a leave of absence.

When we get back to the apartment, Helen grabs a Hefty trash bag—a huge one, though not as big as the one Mort was in on the newsreel—and she collects all the flower arrangements that I've been letting decompose.

While she's occupied, I start packing, and I decide to pick off Lola's medicine cabinet. Like the petals of a daisy: I *need* it, I need it *not*, I need it *now*, I'll need it *later*. Valium, Librium, anything with a white label and a note of caution. None of it will be any good to her anymore anyway. But when I open the medicine chest, anticipating a pharmaceutical jackpot, the cupboard is bare. Somebody beat me to it.

This is the form our sibling rivalry takes.

On a warm July morning, six weeks after the accident, Ben and Helen drop me at the airport to begin my journey back to Paris. Then they drive Lola to a hospital in Massachusetts, a place we call "rehab" to bolster our morale. Braintree Institute is appropriately named, connoting a nice firm cerebral trunk, designed to soak up mental nutrients and push out leafy masses of gray matter. This is where our mother, a fifty-five-year-old woman whose IQ was north of a 150 before she smoked the boat's tailpipe, is supposed to graduate from diapers. No one has suggested she can learn to walk again or to speak coherently. She has only to be able to press the call button, to get an attendant to wheel her to the potty without incident. That is our whole family's new life goal—a life without Wet Ones—so that after graduation she can get into the best nursing home money can buy, the kind where she will shuck off her Pampers and wheel herself into the bathroom.

Just after dawn, my plane drops through the morning fog

over Paris, flying low over perfect rectangles of corn. Before breakfast, I'm back in my apartment, and I head out for a run through the woods in the Bois de Boulogne. I jog around the sapphire lake and take the little ferry to Napoleon's café, where I'd been inhaling hyacinth and croissants in May, just before getting Ben's call about the disaster. Sitting on the terrace, in the shade of the spreading chestnut trees, I sip espresso and devour a basket of *pain au chocolat*. I'm under strict instructions "to resume my life"—as though I'd left it on pause and could return to it now, find my mark, and press play.

Cue the shopping, the chèvre, the châteaux.

TWELVE

Unrequited Love

Back in the City of Light, after absorbing condolences for Mort, I've been mute about what's happened to Lola, unable to say out loud that the death for which everyone is so genuinely sorry was the prelude to a disaster beyond consolation. Work is a useful distraction, conducted in the finest restaurants, and I go through the motions of the *grand cru* life. But the illuminated monuments go unnoticed while my mind marks time in another zone, the scrim around me thicker than the morning fog in the French countryside. Not even that revered remedy for *la morale*, champagne, pierces my indifference.

Moreover, France is in the *merde*. Terrorists have shot up the synagogue on rue Copernic and bombed Rosenberg's Deli in the Marais. Blowing up the Jewish quarter is an old French tradition, but last month someone bombed Le Grand Véfour, which has the most aristocratic dining room in Paris—and that got everyone's attention. In the run-up to New Year's, champagne popping and oyster shucking can't mask the national mood disorder—existentialism—and I have no resistance. Under pale skies, the city is wan, wet, and gloomy, and the natives turn lazier and pricklier and more philosophical.

I bicker, therefore I am.

Walking through the quiet streets of my mannered neighborhood or on a path in the gardens nearby, I sometimes spot an old woman with white gloves, coarse white hair, and soft round shoulders, not one woman really, but many, with a cane or a walker, alone or attended, and a curtain parts. I want to help her cross the street. I want to scoop up dog poop before she steps in it. I want to pull her close and feel her loose skin around me and crawl into her lap and go to sleep. The mighty god of love, who always looked the other way when my mother's arms were open, has cast a spell on me now that they've slammed shut.

Lola used to have an uncanny ability to ferret out the neediness in my girlfriends. Right away, she could spot the ones who were insecure, and almost as soon as they were introduced, she'd put an arm around them and confide, "You're just like a daughter to me." She confessed this feeling nearly indiscriminately to almost every one of them, from the time I was in kindergarten until I got out of grad school, and she said it within moments of a first meeting. Of course they all loved her. But I was mortified by her instant intimacy—not least because her motivation was transparent. I knew it was my mother who needed to be loved, and that was because I was unable to love her. She needed someone to be "just like a daughter" to her.

Melancholy is a cozy armchair in France, and I can't think of a better place to mourn. The natives exult in misery, so glamorous in their gloominess that they parse it into ennui and malaise. Piaf's heartbreak streams from every café and Camus's

The Stranger has been a best seller for four decades. *Mother died today*—the opening sentence speaks to me in an unexpected way each time I think of it. Meanwhile, my huge hoard of childish fury is dissolving into thick lumps of sadness and mucus and guilt. *This* is mal de mère.

Nights when I can't sleep, I jump into my dented Austin Mini and drive up and down the Champs-Elysées with Nina Simone moaning lonesome love songs through my tape deck. Nothing is bleaker than her six stanzas of "Ne Me Quitte Pas." Down the quais, past the Louvre, around the obelisk, around and around the Arc de Triomphe I drive, until the carousels stop turning, until the lights go out on the Eiffel Tower, until the last café in Montmartre closes. And then I go to work.

"What's happening in the Stink-o test market? Where's the new ad campaign?" That's what the client kept asking during my home leave. But the deadlines *whooshed* by unobserved while the French rites of idleness rose phoenix-like from the ashes of my American work ethic.

My team was too busy cogitating to do anything, owing to their strict adherence to the Cartesian method—procrastination, nitpicking, negativity, fastidiousness, and sloth. Descartes's seminal achievement was erecting an unbridgeable divide between mind and matter. Mind is that which thinks but cannot move. Matter is that which moves but cannot think. Mind and matter are so different from each other that interaction between them is inconceivable. Unfortunately, this is just a logical step away from lassitude and the thirty-five-hour workweek (the Socialists' seminal achievement three hundred years later). Foreseeing this quandary, Descartes grudgingly allowed that mind and body could interact through the pineal gland. That's how to get things accomplished.

I don't know much about the pineal gland, but in French people, it's way too small.

Meanwhile, our client has been paying the trade generously for every stick, spray, and roll-on they've agreed to stock—a "discount" that's called "bribery" in other countries. And so in September, our team of four takes a week on the Riviera, the site of our test market, to motivate the two dozen mom-and-pop stores on the scenic roads between Antibes and Monaco, driving back and forth across the steep Corniches where Grace Kelly went over the edge barely a year ago.

Between store checks, we squeeze in white truffles in Eze and langoustines at the Moulin de Mougins. In Saint-Paul, white doves turn golden as the sun sets above our table at La Colombe d'Or. Under Reagan, the dollar is trading at ten francs, and all of France is like Filene's Bargain Basement.

The test market looks like a total disaster, but it will take six months before anyone at headquarters will have numbers to prove it. In the interim, we return to Paris and fete ourselves with Veuve Cliquot and numbered ducks at La Tour d'Argent.

I am promoted, fait accompli, and named deputy head of Pan-Europeanism. In my new role, as Pan, I am to spin BS like cotton candy, out of sugar and air and over wider geography, with phrases that are redolent and sticky, but meaningless.

This isn't as easy as it sounds.

My job is to "shift" Pan-European attitudes. "I'm supposed to make the French adjust their attitude?" I ask my boss when he visits from New York.

"Exactly. First the French, then the Brits and the Krauts." He pats me on the back and gives me his usual pep talk. "Americans make the best Europeans. Don't screw up."

So I develop an insufferable speech to inspire the creative teams, "The Deodorant Brand as a Person," as though it's Eliza

Doolittle and they're Henry Higgins, and I spread it across the continent like melted mozzarella. I lug my overhead to our offices in all the major cities like a debutante on a European tour. Sleeping under a fresh down quilt at the Hotel Sacher in Vienna, devouring Sacher torte and muddy coffee after *Don Giovanni* at the opera. I'm in Rome just long enough to spread the marketing gospel at the Hotel Hassler and sip Bellinis at Harry's—with Leonard Bernstein at the next table. Then off to Villa d'Este to give a pep talk on "The Future of Antiperspirancy."

The client is like my rich uncle, so welcome is my sanctioned propaganda on the virtues of something the home office trademarked Brand Soul—"*Who is your Brand? What is its essence? Where is the love?*"—a manifesto that plagiarized equally from Plato and Roberta Flack, anthropomorphizing our beloved denture adhesives and toilet-bowl cleansers and powdered orange-juice substitutes.

While I drift across Europe, Ben and Helen take turns visiting Lola in rehab, labeling her drawers with words she can read but can't understand—*panties, comb, toothbrush*. She doesn't recognize them. Hasn't in months. And when she speaks about children, all she says is, "Kids are no good." Generalized but specific. She doesn't have to say it directly, because we know what she means: Her kids stuck her in an institution and left her there.

"Lock her up and throw away the key," she says when they come to visit.

Ten times a day, Lola tells a nurse, "Call Nancy, call Nancy." But when I get her on the phone, she has no idea who I am.

"Diminished-density effect," someone tells me.

Such a rare neurological curiosity is she, so intoxicating is "the delayed onset of encephalopathy," that experts have been lining up, begging to be assigned to her case for a glimpse of the potholes on her neurological highway. Nothing can be done to repave her cerebral asphalt—"What's done is done"—but mapping the damage is its own reward. Shaking their heads solemnly in unison, the doctors pinpoint the latest gaps in her MRI and make confident predictions about what's next. They're sure they know which way her brain is headed; they just can't say how long it will take to get there. Lola's gray matter is so instructive, they plan to pose it as a final-exam question, publish it, and maybe light it up like a Broadway show.

The subject of all this attention can't follow a two-step command like "Sit down and take off your shoes." She slices and dices language like a Cuisinart and talks about herself in the third person, as though her "I" is gone.

"She's hungry. She pooped. Get her dinner."

She reads aloud incessantly, but she reads in a monotone, without understanding a word she's saying, whether she's reading a cereal box, a phone book, or *Good Housekeeping*. She reads English the way I read Hebrew, able to recognize the letters and make the sounds, but with no clue what the words mean or how they connect. Her mind, which was a prism, is now a cul-de-sac.

"A-*pha*-sia," Dr. Greely yells at me over the phone. "UH-*FAY*-ZHIA," as though I'll get it if he says it louder, the way people scream directions at foreigners.

"Where is the blockage? Is the problem comprehension or expression? Do her words get scrambled on the way in or on the way out?"

"Both, probably."

This "probably" is not an invitation to probe; it's the kind of "probably" that means "definitely."

Lola has Wernicke's aphasia—no surprise, it's not your everyday aphasia—it's a rare ability to speak fluently without comprehension, pitch, or emotion. And so she spends her days earnestly parroting back gibberish. Which is not so different from how I spend my days. In her case, this is called "dementia." In mine, it is called "spin," because my gibberish builds up meaning, like layers of flavor in a fine sauce.

What do words *mean*? Lola's words are stripped down, but they form English sentences. Unfortunately, the sentences bear no relation to any reality outside of her own mind. Everything she says is self-referring; and yet, since she never speaks in the first person, there may be no actual "self" there, either. I am completely confused.

"The bottom line is demyelinization," Greely loves to say.

His sentences are as hard to parse as Lola's, but he boils it down for dummies: The coating that protects the nerves is as delicate as the membrane on an egg—and hers is fried—so she's as likely to be put back together again as Humpty-Dumpty.

Even if the family is very, very persistent and the patient was once very, very smart, even if she still has a little Gamatria left in her, even if her son is a doctor, the brain does not regenerate.

But why not?

In high school biology, I trained a planarian, a flatworm with two crossed eyes in the center of its pin-size head. Before my coaching, the planarian whiled away the day sucking haphazardly around a petri dish. But with guidance, mine learned to suck to the right whenever I shined a light. In week three, I followed a recipe to split its symmetrical body in half with a scalpel, taking care to divide its crossed eyes evenly, even though both of them were staring at the blade the whole time, and after a respectable period of regeneration, both clones turned right in my spotlight. This was a remarkable experiment, one whose benefits to the planarian are lost on me, but it taught me that you never know what's really going on inside anything, even a single-celled creature. And it prepared me to shine a metaphorical light on my mother's mental petri dish, until all of her brain cells get ready to turn in the right direction.

So I tiptoe into her mind by phone almost every night, which is pointless, but hearing my mother chatter meaninglessly makes me feel connected, or at least as connected as we're likely to be. Except for the pleasantries of a nurse who answers and hangs up, at my mother's end there is only gibberish. And although I was rarely drawn into her lifelong speed talking before the accident, her jabberwocky is a siren song that enthralls me now.

Some nights, the nurses tell me, Lola hums "Makin' Whoopee" for hours. Occasionally, she hums while I'm talking to her, and I sing along.

Picture a little love nest
Down where the roses cling
Picture the same sweet love nest
Think what a year can bring.

I marvel at her disposition—her gentleness, her sweetness, her, dare I say it, lovableness—this woman I mistook for a monster and treated like one. Whose life voyage was launched with what Bill made her do and finally ran aground in Mort's perfect storm.

"That's nice," she says, for no reason at all, all of the time, and the world would be a better place if this caught on.

Before Christmas, I met an architect while I was skiing with friends in Val d'Isère. Jacques had a craggy face and a sunbaked smile that said, *Oui*. At dinner that first night in a candlelit bistro, it snowed while we talked for hours over wine and raclette. The conversation stretched my French vocabulary, but except for a word here and there, I thought I got the gist of it. Anyway, the most basic thing was his smile—even though the cultural dissimilarities were evident from the moment he said *bonjour.*

He smoked, a terrible habit, he admitted.

And I thought, So what. He'll quit.

He lived with another woman, he told me.

And I thought, So what. She'll move out.

He was a *partouzeur,* he told me, and then he winked.

When he went to the men's room, I asked a friend, "what's a *partouzeur?*"

She blushed. "He's a swinger."

And I thought, Great, I like jazz, too.

It didn't take Jacques long to provide a more pointed translation, and even though Lola would have loved him, he was not for me. In the dreary monastic shell of my current existence, the climax is the sound of a nurse disengaging the phone from my mother's ear and putting it back into its transatlantic cradle after she's hummed a few bars of "Makin' Whoopee."

So on my thirty-sixth birthday, six months after my return to Paris and eight months after Mort's mortal misadventure, I'm eating take-out pheasant from the local rotisserie, with Stink-o on my mind, when my sister calls with a major update.

Helen's at the end of her leave of absence, staying in a motel near Braintree. Despite her recent conversion to Roman Catholicism, she's been rounding up a minyan of ten Jewish men every night at the tiny Braintree Synagogue—as part of a child's duty to get a dead parent properly received in heaven. Apparently, Helen inherited the gene for religiosity, whereas I knew way back in Hebrew school that I couldn't make the leap of faith across the parted Red Sea.

Today, she tells me, she filed paperwork to declare Lola legally incompetent and appoint Ben as guardian—a post for which there's been no sibling rivalry. Helen goes into great detail about something called a "bill of incompetency," which sounds like, but isn't, executive clemency—it's more like Miranda rights for the mentally disabled. And then she tells me that's not the point anyway. The point is something called a "lacunar infarct," which sounds like, but isn't, an eclipse of the moon—although it is an eclipse of the brain, a dead hole in the cortex. Lola's been having more of them—more Wite-Out in her gray matter, more *permversability*—which is not a good thing. Months after being gassed, her brain injuries keep growing, like a corpse's hair.

Happy birthday.

While I've been celebrating with Stink-o and relentlessly grinding my way up to the middle, Lola has been regressing in rehab. According to Helen, Lola's begun to walk in reverse. "Parkinsonian retropulsion," Helen "explains" over the phone—it's like stuttering, she tells me, only with the body, and backward.

It occurs to me that this might be a cryptic gesture on Lola's part, that maybe she's trying to rewind herself—to reverse the irreversible. That would be so like her, to "Begin the Beguine," but in code, like her counting to *chai* at Shady Tree. Could she be taking *eighteen* little backward steps? I wonder. Has Helen been counting?

Yes, of course Helen has been counting, she assures me. She had a planarian of her own.

Leaving aside her neurological vernacular—the "left-hemisphere degeneration" and the "basal-ganglia hemorrhaging" and the "extrapyramidal syndrome"—the bottom line is summarized in a "progress" report from Lola's cognitive therapist, which Helen reads me over the phone:

" 'This fifty-six-year-old widow can't list the recent presidents, thinks it's 1937 or 1968, can't sort shapes or colors, and doesn't know the difference between a pen and a quarter. She talks incessantly in cocktail party cadence, with no apparent content or comprehension. And she doesn't know her name.' "

"We knew all that," I tell Helen. "What about the toilet training?"

"Not his department."

So the next day, she makes an unannounced trip to the institute, where potty training is the full-time curriculum—where Lola is supposed to be learning to press the call button and say "Poop" and really, truly mean it—but when Helen arrives, she finds Lola tied to a chair in a hallway and festooned in a Pamper full of excrement.

Thus confirming the *beyond hopelessness* of it all.

Restraining Lola in her Geri-Chair is standard operating procedure, a nurse explains, only slightly embarrassed. This patient needs to be tied up for her own safety. "It's written right into her chart, see? She's a danger to herself."

As Helen recounts this story to me, I have no trouble imagining Lola dangerously unrestrained, moseying in reverse through other patients' rooms, falling backward into their beds. But Helen, being Helen, made ugly litigious noises and dug in until a doctor revised the order in Lola's chart. And Helen will stay on the case until Lola gets all the supervised potty training that's coming to her. Until she gets to the final punctuation at the end of the sentence that started with the "comma" she wasn't expected to survive in the first place.

In the meantime, I brush aside the neurological *fantasy echo*. Ben and Helen speak it fluently, but it's Celtic to me.

Dyslogia, dyspraxia, disaster.

Despite my limited neurological training, we all share a desire to decipher Lola's jabberwocky. On the phone with her, I spend hours talking about nothing with someone who doesn't know *she* is there, never mind that *I* am. If that's not solipsism, I don't know what is. And yet I'm hooked on it, convinced there must be a way to get inside her head and make sense of what she means. She talked to me plenty when all I could say was "goo-goo." So now it's my turn. I savor her nonsense as though the gibberish is a riddle, jam-packed with codes.

The Greeks insisted it was impossible to *talk* about nothing. Talking about nothing is no talk at all. If you're talking, it must be about *something*. Right? Well, maybe. Since Lola's talking, maybe it means there's someone inside her head. Maybe we're talking about something that she understands. Or maybe not. Maybe I'm talking to myself and she has no more self to talk to. I don't know. How could I *know*?

But I hope.

I hope even though I'm a registered skeptic. I hope even though hope is counterproductive. I hope because *the thing with feathers* soars above the boundary of reason. It flouts empirical evidence and expert judgment and even *permversability*.

We believe what we need to believe, no matter how cultivated our skeptical principles. I believe that Lola's graduation from coma to echolalia to *fluent* aphasia is progress. That's how it looks to me, and to Ben and Helen, too. We are the Aphasia Hope Society. Lola's puzzling phrases might turn out to be cryptograms. *Who knows?* The ordinary ramblings of an aphasic, when it's your aphasic, can seem exotic.

But hope gets no traction at Braintree. Families read into things, the experts tell us; that's only normal. "Consensual validation" is the first thing they call it, then "folie à deux," and, when they realize there are three of us, "sibling syndrome." The last is a concept we all rather like.

Time will tell, Ben says.

Not that I've confessed this to anyone but Dr. Greely, but I believe that Lola has a private language, and sometimes, late at night, especially after I've had a glass or two of wine, I can sort of channel it over the phone. It's nothing definitive, just a feeling.

Greely doesn't buy a word of it.

"There are no private languages," he tells me. "If it's a language, it's not private. And if it's private, it's not a language."

Sometimes, Greely sounds just like Wittgenstein; other times, he sounds like a crank.

"It *is* true that she's jocular," he acknowledges grudgingly, "but in a frontal lobe–like manner."

Whatever that means.

But at least he notices—Lola's mind may lack torque, but her heart is a cheerful rudder. Pollyanna meets Goofy—and I am smitten.

My mother is finally the center of my universe now. My love is as wide as the ocean that separates us, and that is its depth and its strength—denial floating on distance.

Accidents change everything.

Eleven months after the disaster, it's April in Paris, when it rains a little every day. After a long dialectic on the meaning of nothing, Dr. Greely has tamped down my optimism like the coals of a dead fire, although Ben and Helen have yet to fold. After my morning jog-cum-cholesterol-festival, the phone rings, and it's Ben, sounding, uncharacteristically, like Jiminy Cricket.

Lola, he announces, just called him by name on the phone. She called him by *his* name—his *own* name—for the first time since the accident. And that's all it takes to convince him that she's really, really beginning to organize her thinking now. "The fog is definitely lifting. Time will tell how much."

From this scant information, delivered in my brother's usual convincing tones, I leap to the hasty conclusion that Lola's complete recovery is finally on its way.

Braintree brushes him off, immune by now to our "anecdotal

evidence." Sooner or later, someone points out to Ben, even a parrot would get his name right.

But after a month of research and a little medical serendipity, Ben turns up proof—an article that has just been published in Japan about a handful of miners who survived carbon-monoxide poisoning, and then, about six months after their own "commas," began to show modest signs of neurological recovery. True, none of the men has rushed back to work just yet—but at least they've begun to feed themselves. And they're continent.

By the time Ben gets the full text translated, Lola's beginning to prove the same things at Braintree: She's pointing to what she wants, trading in her air piano for a toy xylophone, and, most important, she's pressing the call button. The call button is Lola's specialty. She pushes it at the slightest premonition of a movement, and all of Braintree is on colon duty, no contraction too small to ignore.

And so the rehabilitation begins. Lola rides slowly back up the hill she so rapidly descended. Standing, balancing, and her first few unsteady steps. Her speech is still a tossed word salad, but a therapist gave her a box of word blocks—which bypass the brain's speech center—and her thoughts come tumbling out in stanzas that are clear enough for a candy striper.

bed is wicked
I screaming here
free everything.

Even brain-damaged, Lola thinks in haikus.

Later, when she's finally able to talk meaningfully—and is willing to talk about her time in captivity—this will be all she'll say: Tied to a chair, screaming silently, she sensed the word on the tip of her tongue. Being able to say "poop" was all she hoped for.

Then one day, as if from nowhere, she remembered teaching the word to me, and out it came.

She'd been both teacher and student of potty words, but finding the right vocabulary the second time around was tougher than learning it the first. Apparently, it's a lot easier to develop your natural talents than to rebound from the loss of them.

THIRTEEN

The Second Coming

ONE YEAR AFTER THE ACCIDENT
MAY 1984

At 53,000 feet, the Concorde glides seamlessly into Mach 2, breaking a barrier no one can feel. The stewardess deposits "a smoked salmon roll-up on a crème fraîche pillow" onto my linen-lined tray and pours me a glass of Meursault. The air, and everything else, is finer up here, and from the window, I can see the curvature of the earth. Good for Columbus. I never would have figured it out.

Henry Kissinger is in the front row, just ahead of me, correcting proofs of his latest book with a fist-size Mont Blanc pen. I can't resist strolling by—multiple times—peeking at his opus while holding up a prop to attract his attention, a medical text I'm studying for home leave—*Sequelae of Severe Traumatic Brain Injury*. Henry doesn't even look up.

The doctors are calling Lola's case "a recovery that defies medical explanation." I don't think she defied medical explanation so much as she upended a few of its wrongheaded assumptions. Lola contradicted the most fundamental things her neurologists were certain they knew about brain-tissue death, confirming my suspicion that *nothing is permversable*, especially "knowledge."

You can only really know a thing, I'd argued in Philosophy 101, if the thing itself is unchangeable. Because if the thing that you thought you knew suddenly changed, you could hardly be said to have known it. A year after her accident, while I'm flying toward her, Lola is proving that Plato was right.

She's turning in her adult Pampers, getting up out of her wheelchair, and walking out of the hospital. She'll be on furlough, though, having been prescribed "two weeks at home with children." This will be her audition. And we are just what the doctor ordered.

She won't be herself, Dr. Greely warned me over the phone. Maybe that's good news, I can't help thinking, torn between my blind love for the unknown, new Lola and my practiced fear of the old one. I've learned from cramming studies in the fat medical text that I should expect impairments in her attention, memory, concentration, behavior, cooperation, judgment, impulse control, motor control, and mood.

> *And what rough beast, its hour come round at last,*
> *Slouches towards Cranston to be born?*

There's no one to meet me at the airport, since Ben and Helen are checking Lola out of Braintree and making her first wish come true (the beauty parlor). I rent a car and drive through the historic section of Providence. Crossing the river and heading up College Hill, I see a pocket of bohemian renewal spreading around Brown University. Eighteenth-century Colonial homes have been converted into galleries and boutiques that sell one-of-a-kind tie-dyed T-shirts and hammered-silver earrings. Today's special at the deli on Thayer Street is pita stuffed with tofu and alfalfa sprouts. Change is abundant, and irresistible.

On Westminster Street, Max Geller is outside his clothing store, hanging a sale sign, but I don't slow down or even wave. When I was in high school, Lola wasn't sure whether she'd had an affair with Max or had just wished for it. There was a time when she was sure of it; she was so sure that she'd confessed it to everyone, but the result was such a quick and spectacular dose of shock therapy that her original certainty faded into something like a vague and painful yearning. Now I doubt she'd even know his name.

Downtown has fallen into seedy disrepair, the site of abandoned jewelry factories and boozy watering holes where Monty, my grandfather, once passed his nights (and days). The rabbi's dilapidated house on Main Street was torn down years ago, bulldozed, paved over, and turned into a Goodrich parking lot. But around the corner on Doyle Avenue, the three-story tenement where Nana lived with Monty is still standing—despite being "dynamited a little" in the twenties. This was the site of their still during Prohibition, their poker parlor in the thirties, a Green Stamp operation that I never understood during my childhood, and a bookie joint that lasted until I left for college.

After installing a dozen telephones in the parlor, Nana rigged foot cranks, which inverted the telephone stands and revealed sewing machines bolted to the other side. By the time a visitor climbed up to the third floor, he'd find a bunch of old ladies sewing industriously, just a cozy little sweatshop. She'd pull a curtain over the chalkboard where she recorded the bets, and if Lola was around, Nana would make her stand in front of it for a minute to memorize the numbers and then wipe it down. Leave it to my grandmother to brag about an unethical cover for an illegal operation.

Nana may have tried to throw herself into Monty's grave at his funeral, but while he was alive, they threw themselves at each other—hurling insults mostly, but not exclusively—words filled with saliva and accompanied by spitting. Inadvertent spitting, I think.

"Litvak," he called her.

"Rushchacha chalaria," she screamed back.

"Meshuggeh!"

"Palooka!"

"Narish!"

"Goylem!"

I didn't know what half the words meant, but they sounded exotic, and I always thought she was right, no matter what she said.

They moved in with us two or three times a year, when Mort and Lola went on the road. Mort was trying to sell Bobbie Pin Genie and Finesse up and down I-95, and Lola went with him whenever she'd been "under too much pressure"—their road trips being the last stop before Shady Tree. Nana worked the night shift at the rubber factory and Monty spent his days at the dog track. He showed up for dinner with "Nana's paper," *The Racing Daily*, after which he drank beer and whiskey until he was pickled and potted, until he was blotto, stink-o and tanked, and then he went downtown for a nightcap before she had to leave for work.

One night during dinner when I was about eight, Monty ran out of words, and his old boxer's instincts got the better of him. Our grandfather, who was the national featherweight champion in 1921, whose hands were classified as lethal weapons, lifted our grandmother up from her chair and pinned her against our kitchen wall. He gave her a swift right hook to the stomach, which knocked the brisket out of her, and a frothy gray substance leaked out of the corners of his own mouth. It was probably just mashed potatoes and gravy, but he looked like a mad dog, and he was growling.

"I'll kill ya, Leah. This time, I'm really gonna kill ya."

He was very convincing.

As the eldest, it was my duty to mount a defense. "Get off her, you bum," I screamed. I knew he was a bum, because it was the one thing everybody could agree on. I was scared he'd kill me, too, of course, but he just swatted me away like a mosquito and concentrated on the task at hand—killing my grandmother.

Ben, who weighed about thirty-five pounds at the time, jumped off the kitchen table and onto Monty's back and rode him like a bronco, kicking him and slapping the side of his head. It's doubtful that Monty had any feeling left in his head after his years in the ring, and the slapping barely slowed him down. But I bit his legs as hard as I could, and Helen, who was four, jumped up and down and screamed out the window. We could always count on Helen to scream. We were a team.

"Get out of our house, you palooka," I commanded, mustering all the bogus authority I could feign. And something finally stopped him, or else he'd just had enough, and he stumbled off her and grabbed his filthy trench coat and staggered out the back door, a quarter inch of plate glass, which I slammed and locked for effect. "And don't come back."

Nana collapsed, gagging, but not for long. She pulled herself up and announced we were all going out to play bingo even though it was a school night. And not just *any* bingo, but the BIG one in Pawtucket. We never discussed the attempted homicide, and I never told anyone the story. The only protection I could give Nana was her privacy.

Years later, after she died, I asked my mother if she'd ever seen Monty hit Nana, pretending the question was rhetorical.

"Sure," Lola said. "He hit her all the time."

"Then how could you leave your children with him?"

"He'd *never* hurt you kids."

I wasn't so sure about that, so I told her the dream I'd been having for years about Monty. Ben and I are tiny, two and four, all alone, wading in the bay in front of our summer cottage in Narragansett, being very careful not to go in above our belly buttons. Then Monty comes running into the water like a mad dog, only he's dressed in his brown striped suit and city shoes, and he grabs Ben and pushes him under a wave.

"That was no dream," Lola said; "that was the truth. Only Monty didn't push Ben under; he pulled him out."

My mother was willing to admit that my awful recurrent nightmare was actually the truth, but she wanted to rewrite the ending. Classic Lola.

"I left you at the edge of the water because the baby was crying in the house. I was only there a minute when Monty pulled up in his car and looked down to the beach and saw a wave wash over the two of you and drag you both under. He went running down those steps and into the water without even taking off his shoes. You kept screaming, 'Don't drown my brother,' when it was Monty who saved him. Actually, he saved *both* of you. He yelled at me for a week after. Maybe he blamed me for what happened."

"Maybe," I said.

Lola would have been twenty-four, with two toddlers and an infant screaming in a crib. Plus a bout, no doubt, of postpartum depression.

And then I remembered the rest of my "dream"—my heels slipping in the sand, my head going underwater, thrashing at Monty with an empty milk bottle in my hand. "How could the bottle have been empty if it was underwater?" I used to ask my shrink. "It's a symbol," he always replied; "you have to figure it out." I never did. But at last I could see it clearly—it wasn't a symbol after all; it was Ben's leakproof baby bottle.

In the little garden outside Lola's apartment complex, pink azalea and rhododendron are at the end of their blooms, and roses are puckered up. Inside, withered masses of botanic decay are lined up in the hallway, ready for execution. No one has been in her place for months, and the elapsed time has been deadly for the houseplants. But for the rest of us, this is a happy and unexpected homecoming.

Ben and Helen are in the kitchen, dressed like twins in rubber gloves and ragtag aprons, wielding Ajax and Brillo. Lola is napping. But as soon as I put down my luggage, her bedroom door opens and a blonde emerges, someone rested and toned, svelte, and, were it not for the bug-eyed droopiness, she would be beautiful. It's midafternoon, but she's wearing a black cocktail dress with stiletto heels and all her best jewelry. When she comes closer, I smell Lily of the Valley perfume and mothballs.

"I'm happy to see you," she says, holding out her arms. And I believe her, even though she doesn't look happy; she looks dazed. Which is better than the zombie mask, but only just.

I'm happy to see her, too. This is my new mother, and I embrace her as though I've known her my whole life. I'm going to be just like a daughter to her.

While we're celebrating in the kitchen with three glasses of Veuve Cliquot and a ginger ale, the ceiling light blows, and replacing it strikes the three of us simultaneously as a perfect test of Lola's ability to take care of herself. It will be our official test number one. She'll have to perform the entire maneuver on her own, we agree, but we'll be her advisers—a well-published psychologist, a polymath pulmonologist, and a mid-level corporate executive failing up abroad. Collectively, we've traveled four thousand miles to coach this former genius—whose most recent IQ is eighty-nine—on how to change a lightbulb. The answer to *how many* appears to be four.

Ben gives her the rules right away. "The light blew and we'd like you to change it on your own."

She looks at him blankly.

"First, you need to put on sensible shoes, then get the stepladder," he says, taking charge.

"No, she needs to get the lightbulb first," I insist.

"What difference does it make what order she gets them in?" Helen asks.

"Stop fighting," Lola says, her nasal voice a surprise each time I hear it—a monotone, regardless of content.

"We're not fighting," we yell back.

Lola leaves the room.

Helen brings her back wearing flats.

"Okay, let's start again," Helen says in a musical lilt. "And no more nitpicking."

"What should I do first?" Lola asks.

"What do you *think* you should do first?" Helen says.

"I think I should take a nap," Lola replies.

I can see it's counterproductive for a psychologist to be in charge.

"When you wake up from your nap, it will be dark, and there won't be any light in the kitchen," Ben says.

"You've got to think ahead," I add unhelpfully.

"You're giving me a headache," she says.

"Do you want some Tylenol?" Ben offers.

"No, I want a NAP." The word nap comes out louder, but without inflection.

"I don't think she should have Tylenol anyway," I volunteer. "It makes you bleed."

"Tylenol does not make you bleed," he says, exasperated. "And she didn't have a cerebral hemorrhage; it was carbon-monoxide poisoning."

I'm the eldest, so I like to have the last word. "Still," I say, equivocating.

"Let's get it over with already," Lola says. "What should I do first?"

"Get the stepladder," Ben says.

I stand down.

"Where is it?" she asks.

"It's your apartment."

"It was Daddy's stepladder."

"Now it's yours."

Down the hall she shuffles, jiggling various doorknobs. Some she opens; some she just jiggles. Eventually, she finds the stepladder and a bulb and brings them back in two trips that total fifteen minutes. Ben tells her to take the bulb and climb up.

"I can't do both."

"Sure you can," he says ever so solicitously. "You have to hold the bulb so you'll have it when you get to the top step."

"Why can't you hand it to me when I get there?"

"Because I might not be here."

"But you are here."

"Next time, I might not be."

She gets up one step, bulb in hand, and drops it—smithereens.

"I dropped it."

Helen cleans up.

"Okay, start over."

"Why do I have to start over?"

"What would you do if we weren't here?"

"Call the handyman."

"What if he's not there?"

"Wait for him to come back."

Of course she's right, but we're committed. Ben hands her the second bulb, but this time she drops it before getting up the first step—another mess.

"I can't do it. I CAN'T." She clenches her fists and stomps on the crunchy shards like little Shirley Temple having a tantrum.

I am silent, unsure how to motivate her.

"You can do it, Mom. Just try a little harder," Ben says.

"But I won't. I WON'T do it. That's it. I just won't."

And she plods down the corridor to her bedroom and slams the door.

"Good night," we yell simultaneously.

Following the lightbulb preliminaries—which the new Lola failed—the three of us knocked off the champagne without the absorptive benefit of dinner, then stayed up into the wee small hours, like new parents, grading her performance, rolling our eyes, worrying.

Before dawn, noise wakes me, and near the kitchen I hear something dripping. Flipping on the light, I find Lola, wide-eyed as a deer in headlights, wearing a sheer pink negligee and emptying a half-gallon carton of milk into a four-ounce juice glass. The milk is surging over the rim, running off the counter, and bouncing off her formerly fluffy slippers. Nevertheless, she keeps pouring.

"What are you *DOING?*"

"I want some milk."

"But the glass is too small!"

"I don't want very much."

"I mean you're *spilling* it!"

Still, she pours. Nothing has engaged her stop mechanism, not the river flowing off the counter, not the puddle at her feet. I grab the carton—maybe I'm too brusque—because she gives me a look of intense bewilderment, of being very lost in unknown territory. I hand her the glass and she gulps down the milk like a baby, unleashing small slurping noises, her dead doe eyes fixed on me above the rim. Help me, they're saying. Help me. Or maybe they're saying, Leave me alone, I can do it myself. I have no idea what she's thinking.

I sponge the floor around her—and she, so compliant, lifts a foot and leans back against the counter. But in the process, she tips back her glass and dribbles what's left in it down her chin and onto my head.

"Don't worry," she says, "there's more," and she smears a milky trail back to the refrigerator. Lola wants what she wants.

Her will is intact, too strong for me to buck, as it always was, and unfortunately much stronger than her judgment. Maybe that was always true, too. But I've got two weeks to teach her the basics. Holding the carton upside down means it will spill. It's a good idea to turn on a light. A juice glass won't hold a half gallon of milk. Four goes into sixty-four how many times? Basic kitchen catechism. How could a genius who'd once had a photographic memory fail to learn sizes and shapes?

"You should turn on a light, Mom."

"I didn't want to wake anybody."

"But you couldn't see what you were doing."

"I was pouring milk."

"I meant you were spilling because it was dark."

"I spilled because the *bah-ul* is too full."

"If you put the light on, you would have known you were spilling."

"I knew I was spilling."

She refills her glass and lumbers down the hall in her squishy slippers. My tutorial doesn't interest her a bit.

Next stop is the bathroom. She turns the light on—so maybe I am having a small effect—and stares at herself in the mirror the same way she stares at me, at everything: Puzzled, dumbfounded. Stupid-fied, I can't help thinking.

"Aunt Flossie," she says after a while, and it's true. The moon face, the overbite, the Valkyrie curls, these are genes at work. Is she putting it together?

Watching her, it's hard to tell whether Aunt Flossie is one of the connections that was lost in the gas on the boat, or if the resemblance has sparked some insight. Ten minutes pass while she tries to re-form her hair, twisting the phototropic locks she inherited, trying to make them flip under instead of up without benefit of bobby pins or Dippity Doo, but—*surprise!*—they keep doing what they do naturally, again and again. She seems to realize that now—there's no change of expression, no *aha*—but she begins rummaging through the cabinet, looking for something, some agent of change, and I'm rooting for her. She finds a can of mousse and drizzles it over her scalp like frosting, patting down the sticky white foam until it hardens into sticky white crust. It's bad technique, but it will do. Beauty habits die hard, and with luck, they outlast vanity.

After spraying bathroom deodorizer behind her ears, she goes back to bed.

Breakfast is a quiet gathering of the dazed and dehydrated. Lola is the last to appear, wearing Bermuda shorts, as if she's going to the golf course, and pumps, as if she's going to high tea. She's smeared on some makeup over the zombie mask, which doesn't improve it much, even after strong coffee.

"I lost my pearl necklace," she tells us.

"Where'd you last see it?" Helen asks.

"In my bedroom."

"Then look for it there."

"Where should I look for it?"

"In your bedroom."

"How do you know it's there?"

"I *don't* know where it is, but you just told me that's where you last saw it."

"Where did I see it?"

"In your room, you saw it in your room."

"So it's not lost?"

"Yes, it's still lost."

"So YOU look for it."

Helen suggests that Lola clean up the breakfast dishes (a test) as we take cover in the hall, spying as she opens the refrigerator, pushes containers around, finds a few she likes, and then parks herself inside the open door to gnaw on chicken wings and a side of coleslaw. She has brunch there, in the cold, sampling. When she's done, she wipes her face on a kitchen towel, which turns red from lipstick and yellow from chicken fat, and then uses the towel to wipe out the refrigerator.

"We need to go to the market now," she says, apparently to the refrigerator. "We need tuna fish for Pussy."

"You never told her about Pussy?" Helen whispers.

Guilty. I didn't think she'd remember she had a cat. It took her a year to remember she had children.

I go into the kitchen and walk her to a chair and sit her down and face her. "Pussy didn't make it, Mom. I'm sorry."

"He died?"

"Yes, he died at the vet's."

"That's good."

"What's good?"

"I thought he died on the boat."

A beat later, she adds, "But we still need tuna fish."

So we all go out the back door, and Ben holds an umbrella over her head.

"It's not raining," she says.

"It *is* raining," he explains; "the umbrella's keeping you dry."

"I can't feel it."

Ben shuts the umbrella, and rain starts to drip down her forehead.

"It's raining," she says.

"Take the umbrella."

"I can't open it."

"Sure you can. Just try," Ben says.

"I CAN'T." She pushes the umbrella at him.

"I'll show you how to open it," I say in my kindest and most patient voice, which is neither easy nor characteristic. I open and close it three times; then she does it a couple of times herself.

"I can't figure it out," she says.

"But you just *did* it twice."

"I can't figure it out."

She gyrates in the parking lot in her green golf outfit and white pumps, with the umbrella expanding and contracting like a blowfish.

Repetition, repetition, repetition.

How long will it take her to master the concept of *umbrella* and then the broader notion of *preparedness*? How long until she says to herself, "Looks like it's going to rain!" even while she's still in the house, dry, and remembers to grab a raincoat on her way out?

Ben says nothing. He just waits for the learning to occur.

I shine a mental flashlight on our fifty-six-year-old planarian.

The phone's ringing and all three of us run for it, leaving Lola to her umbrella exercises outside. Barely a minute has passed when we hear the collision, the brutal sound of metal crunching metal. I'd forgotten she had a set of keys in her purse.

Although the crash is mercifully brief and not (yet) followed by screaming, by the time I get to the front door and see her behind the wheel of the Buick—next to an overturned mailbox—the car's begun moving again, sideswiping the mailbox a second time. And—while Ben and Helen are running toward her, waving their arms and yelling, "Wait! Not yet! Slow down! Stop!"—she runs over it a third time, wedging it under the chassis. In the blink of an eye, she's turned the Buick into a bulldozer.

Ben calls for a tow truck, and Helen gives me the keys to Mort's Caddy. "Don't put the tuna in the trunk," she reminds me.

Later that day, Lola's current neurologist squeezes us in without an appointment. A rheumy-eyed graybeard in a huge wood-paneled office decorated with diplomas, he invites Ben, Helen, and me into his consult room while Lola waits at the reception desk.

"Well, she has very little depth perception," Dr. Moore tells us without giving her an eye exam. "She can't judge the distance between objects."

"That's not so bad, is it?" I say. "Or do you think it's a symptom of something worse?"

Ben and Helen look at me like I'm an idiot.

"It's a symptom of *brain damage*," Dr. Moore says, reminding us of Lola's *permversability*. "She shouldn't drive."

Lola lives in a suburb, where driving is as important as pressing the call button. I look at Helen for help, but her rosy cheeks are pale.

"Lola needs a caretaker," Moore adds.

Her recent history flashes before me in short clips, the highlights of her near accidents and small accidents since the big accident. She can't climb a step stool or change a lightbulb or pour milk or open an umbrella without assistance. The new Lola is as willful and stubborn as the old Lola, though the new one is like Bambi caught in cross fire. And this one can't drive.

"Maybe I'll just take her home for a while," I say.

"To Paris?" Ben says. "You think she's going to learn French?" he adds, like a heckler.

I close my eyes and imagine Lola showing up on the *rue* where I live—her zombie mask tucked under a beret. A lifelong insomniac with jet lag, she wanders while I work. She gets shortchanged at the *banque*, lost in the *Métro*, overdosed at the *pharmacie*. She pleads for help from my concierge, Madame Pas Maintenant. She falls down the laundry chute, off the Eiffel Tower, into the Seine, floating, facedown, like Ophelia.

"You have to deal with the fact that your mother is brain-damaged," Moore says.

"Brain damage is what she *has*," Helen says. "It's not who she *is*." Helen is our cheerleader.

"I'm not making a moral judgment. This is fact. There are things she can't do. Shouldn't do. Driving is just one of them."

Maybe he's right. It's not like I haven't seen the evidence, wiped up the spilled milk, witnessed the car crash, heard the rusty wheels of her mind grinding between gears. But we're supposed to be the Aphasia Hope Society, and even I, the professional skeptic, who's learned to throw in a hand when my cards are bad, even I am not ready to fold. Maybe Lola needs a warm body to follow her everywhere, carrying car keys, and maybe it won't be happening in Paris, but we've been at this only two days. Can't we give her a chance? There are three of us to manage one of her. Three drill sergeants, three sets of training wheels. We'll give her our best shot, and hopefully we'll all survive.

. . .

And so the reeducation of Lola begins. Over a dinner of Chinese takeout, Ben gives a lecture on the virtues of making lists and establishing priorities. "First things first," he tells her sagely about ten times, although he never quite explains how to figure out what comes first. Meanwhile, Helen nags Lola about her table manners—elbows off the table, don't slouch, don't eat off anyone else's plate. After the spareribs, Helen brings out finger bowls with lemon slices and warm water, which Lola drinks. (Next stop, Maxim's.)

I teach checkbook math to a woman who used to entertain herself doing square roots in her head. Ben takes her to the bank and goes over the concept of deposits. "What deposits?" she asks, and it's true we haven't figured out where the money is going to come from.

I keep an eye on her. We keep six eyes on her. The next night, after kitchen catechism, we go to see *Ghostbusters*. Lola sleeps through the first twenty minutes, exhausted by her culinary indoctrination, and after she wakes up, I stare at her while she stares vacantly at the screen.

"Did you like the movie?" I ask afterward.

"Yes."

"Did you think it was funny?"

"Yes."

"You didn't laugh."

"Sure I did."

Toward the end of her time in Braintree, with lots on her mind, maybe, but without much vocabulary, Lola began knitting. Since she's been home, she's been working on "something blue" for Ben. The yarn is always at her side in a white plastic garbage bag that crinkles during movies, dinners, and the impromptu concert Ben gives Friday night at the country club. After I shush Lola for making noise, she gets up, looking guilty, and brings

Ben a fluffy pillow so he'll be more comfortable. She walks across the filled room and makes him stand up while he's playing so she can slide a cushion under him. Then she goes back to knitting and crinkling.

The next morning, she produces a skintight navy wool vest with a tiny neck hole and spaghetti straps. Ben tries to model it for her, but he can't get it over his head.

She knows something is wrong but can't figure out what. "The length is good," she says.

"Uh-huh."

"I'll make a pink one for Helen next."

"How about a scarf instead? Or a shawl?" Helen asks.

Something without a neck.

On Saturday, we have our first family foursome, three of us barefoot because we don't have golf shoes (and have never played before), plus Lola, who's decked out like a model from the pro shop in a turquoise number with the club insignia over her heart. She was never a great player, but she was always competitive. Now, however, before she hits the ball, she has to swing at it two or three times until she sort of nicks it. Then she takes a do-over, or two.

When she thinks we're not looking, she moves her ball from the rough to the fairway.

"Two in. Three out. Four even," she says, trying to distract us.

Huh?

"When you put a ball in the water, that's two in. Three out, you're hitting four. Or if it's three, it's three in, four out, hitting five . . . like that."

Other than this new version of Gamatria, she shows no special aptitude for anything on the course except cheating, and her handicap has tripled.

. . .

Sunday, we're invited to a benefit at the Ladies' Jewish Home for the Aged. In the sixties, when Lola was head of the entertainment committee, she decided to liven things up a bit by hiring a sister act Nana recommended (consider the source). Two showgirls, who probably hadn't been on the stage since Coolidge was president, whose pink feathered boas must have leaked flesh even then, tap-danced for five minutes to "Shuffle Off to Buffalo." And then they put on stripper music and took it all off. Shortly thereafter, due to too much pressure, Lola got a dose of the rain hat.

Hours before we're due at the current luncheon, Lola goes to her room to spruce up, and as usual, I keep track from the doorway. I watch her take a green ball gown from her closet, rip a plastic cleaning bag off it, and put it over her head (the plastic bag, not the dress). She pulls the bag over her nose and then over her mouth and pulls it tighter and tighter, until I can't stand it anymore and run into her room, screaming.

"Get that plastic bag off your face!"

She isn't moving—she hasn't passed out or fallen down, but she isn't doing anything to remove the bag—so I poke my fingers through it to keep her from getting asphyxiated, again.

"Stop it. You're messing my hair up."

I rip the bag off her face.

"Whad'ja do that for?"

"Your nostrils were covered!"

"I'm protecting my hairdo."

"You'll suffocate! See?" I wrap the plastic bag around my head, pulling it tight for effect, and I suck in and out dramatically, screaming at her. "*See? See* how I can't *breathe?*"

"You're breathin' just fine. You're talkin', aren't you?"

She pushes me into the hall and shuts her door.

I floss my teeth so hard, my tongue bleeds.

The luncheon "event" is in a threadbare Ethan Allen dining room that holds about a hundred people, and it's crammed with senile old ladies in wheelchairs and overworked caretakers. Everyone is well behaved, except for a lady in the corner who's about ninety-five and keeps yelling, "Take it off! Take it off!" For all I know, she's been cheering nonstop since Lola's strippers performed here twenty years ago.

I'm on my best behavior, determined to sit quietly at a table in the back, dressed in the same Mugler suit I wore at Mort's funeral, with the pinholes from the crepe ribbon still poking out of the silk lapel. Lola's in a slinky green sequined number, one size too small, quick-stepping in her matching green heels, top-heavy and teetering like Bette Midler with her Harlettes.

There's no real entertainment, not the kind Lola used to plan anyway, but Ben is asked to play the piano, and he's always delighted to oblige, grateful for any audience outside of the emergency room. It's an appreciative crowd, and I scan their faces, wishing Sol Hurok could be here to see how Ben turned out. Unfortunately, Sol died in the seventies, without ever having come back to town.

In the center of the room is the gleaming door prize, a ten-gallon jar filled with jelly beans—these are the Reagan years—and the only luncheon drama turns on who will come closest to guessing the number of beans and get to take the jar home. I guess ten thousand, Ben guesses four thousand, and Helen doesn't want to play. None of us has a clue, and *who cares*? Lola cares; that's who.

The bean counter, an elderly woman from Procurement, is drawing out her moment in the limelight. She slaps the microphone with her fist a few times—"Can you hear me?"—then turns up the volume until I'm cringing from the feedback. And then, when the suspense is really unbearable, she announces, "We have a winner, someone who guessed the exact number—6,950 beans! And it's Lola!"

Lola? Our Lola? I haven't heard her count past eighteen in a year.

Stepping up to the microphone, accepting the award on her own behalf, is a woman who has recently demonstrated eight cerebral sequelae of neurotoxicity—impairments in memory, concentration, behavior, cooperation, judgment, impulse control, motor control, and mood. She can't (or won't) open an umbrella or change a lightbulb. She doesn't have sufficient depth perception to hit a golf ball or avoid a mailbox. She knits sweaters with spaghetti straps and can't figure out if it's raining. But Lola hit the jelly bean jar right on the head. *How?* How did she retain this idiot-savant vestige of her old splinter skills?

Maybe I should demand a recount.

Flashbulbs popping, our Queen for a Day throws her arms around the big jar in the center of the dining room and reaches in for her first handful. An enterprising ninety-year-old photographer with a Polaroid offers me a commemorative copy of the moment for just five dollars, and I buy it, like this is Disneyland.

Finally, the party's over, and while we're waiting in front for Helen to bring the car around, Lola's eating jelly beans by the fistful. A button on her coat, which has been straining for days under the pressure of her appetite, pops off and rolls into the driveway, directly into the path of a BMW that's stopping to pick people up. Lola wants her button back, and so she quick-steps over to the Beemer and then bends down, invisible to the driver, who's turned his attention to his passengers. She reaches for the button the way she reached for the garbage disposal, hypnotized and in slow motion, and then, when her hand's in the path of the Beemer's front tire, the car shifts into first.

But coming up swiftly from behind, grunting like a ninja, is

Ben—who knocks over the glass centerpiece, smashing it, so now there are jelly beans everywhere—and he grabs Lola by her sequined collar and yanks her out of thc path of disaster, again.

Unfortunately, with her collar still gripped in his hands, he stumbles over spilled beans and the two of them wind up on the sidewalk.

"Why'd you shove me?" Lola asks, oblivious.

The car runs over her button.

FOURTEEN

Men Are Like Buses

Despite evidence of an emerging splinter skill, after the first week of Lola's home leave, she's survived close calls with her Buick and a Beemer, and it's obvious she's a clear and present danger to herself. The neurologist was right about her needing a caretaker—it can no longer be denied—and in a chance encounter, her savior arrives. Once in a while, life delivers exactly what you need.

Eddie Silverman materializes at Lola's third cousin's grandchild's Bar Mitzvah, a garish affair for three hundred in the Biltmore Hotel downtown. He's the only available man in the room over thirteen—deus ex machina in a gray polyester leisure suit—and Lola picks him up like a goody bag. In her black-and-white polka-dot dress, she stalks him at the buffet, sits down next to him at his table, spreads honey on her challah and gives him a little nibble, and, after spinning him around in the hora, bear-hugs him to klezmer music for the rest of the evening.

"Men are like buses," Lola loved to say. "Miss one, hop on another." Even in her current condition, she's a bus stop. A man magnet. Eddie doesn't stand a chance.

He's seventyish, good-looking, with broad shoulders, no potbelly, a full head of white hair, and the cranky disposition of an army sergeant. She tells me, "He used to be a big shot in air-conditioning." I'm guessing he was a repair guy. She brings him home for dinner three nights in a row. I serve up coq au vin, rack of lamb, and salmon poached to perfection. Though they've known each other less than a week, he badgers her like they've been married a lifetime.

"Stand up straight. Put the cap back on the soda bah-ul. You don't need a second dessert. Stand up straight. Stop eating already. Turn on the damn light."

He's perfect.

By the end of the week—the end of her furlough—when the music stops and it's time for all the contestants to find a chair or get tossed from the game, Eddie and Lola hold hands and announce that they're moving to Florida together. Sure, it's fast, but Eddie says he's a quick judge of character. He may have been married three times, but he's been divorced only once. His first two wives died young, he explains, looking for the sympathy vote. No doubt they were bullied to death.

He knows somebody who knows somebody who has a sublet in West Palm. He scraped together the deposit money from his Social Security checks, and Lola wants to throw in some of Mort's insurance legacy, and it all adds up to a three-month rental. A compatibility test. He's certainly no charmer, but he's eager enough, and apparently the flesh is willing. If the flesh weren't willing, Lola would never throw money into the pot.

Unfortunately, though, his badgering is not limited to her. "Did you make that same goddamn dressing?" he asks me at our last supper, referring to my renowned vinaigrette while pulling a bottle of Wishbone out of his pocket and pouring it liberally over the entire bowl of handpicked mesclun.

Fine. I could give a shit. I'm sick of *him*, too. But Lola likes him a lot better than rehab, and there's no changing her mind. Never has been.

So let them go off together into the sunset over the Intracoastal. Let *him* open her umbrella. Let him nag her to stand up straight and put the cap back on the soda bah-ul. Let him teach her to drive around the mailbox instead of through it. Let him nitpick her back to mental health.

Repetition, repetition, repetition.

In an unspoken toast, I award Eddie the metaphorical flashlight I used to train my planarian. And then I reserve a seat back to Paris.

"Thank God," Helen says the minute we're alone, "we've been spared."

All night long, the theme song from *Rocky* plays in my head and keeps me from falling asleep. We're having a miracle here. The Messiah has driven up to Lola's bus stop in a red convertible Pontiac, and she, down on her luck and thumbing in the breakdown lane, is hitching a ride out of town with him—my Get Out of Jail Free card.

Lola may have plenty of handicaps, but still—whatever she wants, she gets. She can't drive, but she just landed a live-in chauffeur. She can't change a lightbulb, but she's got her own electrician. After only two weeks, I was ready to give her limbo stick away to Goodwill, but she's taking it with her to Florida in the trunk of Eddie's Bonneville. He filled up his tank, and now they're going for a ride.

This is the new face of *permversability*.

Before moving on, Lola has to give a deposition in the wrongful-death lawsuit we're pressing against some "deep pockets," starting with the manufacturer of Mort's boat—a company that last saw the vessel fifteen years ago, when it was wheeled out of the factory, brand-new.

Mort found the cabin cruiser secondhand through a broker in Baltimore when it was already ten years old, and he tracked down the owner to buy it from him directly—trying to "cut out the middleman," one of his favorite tactics. He piloted the boat back to Warwick, where he single-handedly maintained it for four years at Folly's Landing. He kept every gas receipt from Cape Cod to Miami, but when our lawyer asked me to search Mort's records, I couldn't find a single bill for maintenance. It was, apparently, the *Mr. Fix It*.

Until recently, there was a statute that limited liability claims against products over ten years old, validating the concept of obsolescence, but in a stroke of great fortune for us, the Supreme Court has just struck it down—making decrepitude a perpetual liability and opening up the floodgates to litigation hell. We get right in line behind Harvey Diamond, our handsome, brilliant tort lawyer. Harvey famously sued the local ashram, which had accepted an heiress's huge trust fund "in exchange for certain promises," and when the heiress was unable to achieve bliss through transcendental meditation, Harvey got her money back—with damages. He's made quite a name for himself winning supersize judgments in what others have called "frivolous" lawsuits. So why not ours?

So what if Mort's boat was fourteen years old? So what if he maintained it on his own, with no assistance, training, or aptitude? So what if his copy of *Piloting, Seamanship, & Small Boat Handling* is still shrink-wrapped? Liability is relative. And we've got Harvey.

To prepare for her testimony, Lola bought a new knit suit, had her hair done, and put on her best pearls. Handsome Harvey and three pinstriped men her age gather around her in a rosewood-paneled conference room in a landmark brick building overlooking the State House. They serve her tea from a silver service, as if she's a visiting dignitary. (Men are like buses.)

A stenographer is brought in and Harvey explains to Lola and me that the cause of Mort's death is not in dispute—the generator leaked carbon monoxide—the question a judge and jury will decide is *who* is to be held responsible for that leak. Harvey thinks the manufacturer should take the rap, for reasons he doesn't bother to explain to us, but he doesn't have to because we're on his side. Nevertheless, he says, gesturing toward the defendants' side of the table, these gentlemen have a few questions about what hand Mort might have played in his own demise. They want to know who maintained the boat, especially the generator. They want to know who replaced the T-joint that connected the generator to the exhaust pipe. And they also want to know who might have allowed that pipe to corrode over a considerable period of time.

Harvey sneers when he says "considerable," as though it's *not* considerable, as though it's less than nothing. I can hardly wait to see him in front of a jury.

Next up is Lola.

Lola. Her memories of the accident and the time leading up to it have vanished during her months in Braintree, and now she has to swear to tell the truth, the whole truth, and nothing but the truth. The very idea of it is almost unthinkable. Even if she *knows* the truth—if she has any inkling of it at all—it would hardly be like the old Lola to tell it. And as for the new Lola—*who knows?*

But before Harvey swears her in, before he gets to the good part, he asks me to leave the room. I'm taken aback by his sense of propriety, having sat through her shrink appointment, her MRI, and her driving lesson, but still, I'm shown the door.

His secretary escorts me to an adjoining office to wait "for about an hour," and I make myself comfortable at Harvey's desk, unable to take my eyes off a huge evidence file that's staring at me. *The Estate of Morton Hornstein versus* a list of defendants so long, it runs off the edge of the label.

Pandora's box.

That box calls to me. But I know once its lid is lifted, what's inside will escape and spread like contagion.

Still, after Pandora lifted *her* lid, after all the evil inside flew out, at the very bottom, she discovered hope. Could there be *hope* at the bottom of this box? Sure, I'm nervous that Harvey will finish up early and walk in on me, but off comes the lid and, *whew,* nothing flies out on its own. Inside, a dozen manila folders, all dressed up and labeled for trial, vie for my attention. I don't have a second to waste, and fortunately, I took speed-reading from Evelyn Wood.

"Exhibit A" is a deposition from the boat's previous owner, an optometrist with 20/20 vision, who swore under oath that he inspected the generator frequently and also had it professionally maintained, and, no, it never showed signs of rusting, it was *maintained,* and, yes, he had the documentation to prove it.

Harvey has no hope of pinning anything on him.

"Exhibit B" is the police report. Salt water had leaked into the bilge compartment, which corroded the generator, and "an improperly replaced T-joint" let carbon monoxide escape. A close-up photo of the T-joint reveals a hole where it met the exhaust, with clumps of rust flaking off it like mud cakes.

Might the mud cakes have been "obvious to the naked eye?"

The next photo, a wide shot, answers that question in the affirmative. One more nail in an already-buried coffin.

Harvey has his work cut out for him.

Sadly, the corroded T-joint isn't the end of the story, even though its layers of rusty buildup must have been years in the making. The automatic start mechanism on the bilge blower was "disengaged," and the fan was "rewired incorrectly." So the carbon monoxide from the generator could not be blown out of the boat by the patented Blow-Matic feature; instead, it gathered in the hold, which was separated from the sleeping berth by a loose hatch.

The operator's manual for the generator is attached, and Harvey has highlighted page fifteen, which has a big black box at the top:

> WARNING:
>
> The Blow-Matic™ is an automatic safety feature for your protection. The blower automatically removes gas vapors, which have deadly and explosive potential.

Below the warning is the blower's official wiring diagram, but unfortunately, next to that is someone's hand-drawn *re*wiring diagram, in which EVERY LETTER OF EVERY WORD IS CAPITALIZED, in ink. Certain words, however, are then crossed out and written over in bigger, bolder caps: START-~~STOP-RELAY-~~AUTO-SWITCH.

Someone blew off the Blow-Matic—which is a seminal example of the kind of jerry-rigging that does not get a do-over.

The police engineer and his crew, donning oxygen masks, with the fire department on standby, started up the generator to measure its gaseous emissions over time. With the Blow-Matic disabled, the dose of carbon monoxide was so concentrated, it would have taken only five minutes to cause headache, ten minutes for dizziness, fifteen for nausea, and twenty for seizures. These milestones have been plotted on a graph, with death as the end point.

As a death machine, the *Mr. Fix It* has few peers. Mort got the more spectacular dose, while Lola's was diluted by sleeping near "a lingering draft from a leaky porthole," which, like the bilge blower, had been repaired "imperfectly." This is why she survived. If Mort had done a better job caulking—if he'd successfully *Mort*-ified the porthole—then Lola would be dead now, too.

The appendix includes twenty-five urgent repairs, most of them marked by black asterisks—I'd have used a skull and crossbones—including more rotting pipes, faulty wiring, and deteriorated parts. The windshield was cracked, the hose to the air conditioner was cut, and the fuel shutoff valve was damaged. It could have caused a fire if the carbon monoxide hadn't killed Mort first.

The instruments of his death must have been lining up for years.

Hand it to Harvey—he blames all this negligence on the manufacturer. Viewed in a litigious context, the boat is a V-shaped gas chamber, a crypt designed to suffocate two, its berth located directly above a defectively devised engine that was housed in a leaky compartment.

The crime report includes signed depositions from various witnesses who found "the victims," including a doctor who climbed through a porthole and was astonished to discover the woman had a pulse. A boat hand wrote how sorry he was that he didn't do more to help the doctor, but it smelled so bad, he threw up over the side. Just as I used to do.

As I'm about to put the files back into the evidence box, I notice a large manila envelope on the bottom—where Pandora found hope. I rip it open in a rush, without thinking, hoping there will be some shred of evidence to exonerate Mort and win Lola her junk lawsuit and a condo in South Beach.

Out spills an eight-by-ten black-and-white glossy of my dead father. And I can't look away. He's on his berth in the fetal position, lying in a regurgitated stew of what was probably steak and potatoes, his hair matted and wild, his knees drawn into his belly, as though he's gone a few rounds with the angel of death and lost. His fists are gnarled like a dead parakeet's claws, and they're clutching at something invisible. His face is a swollen bruise, although the worst of the violence must have been on the inside. And his tongue is hanging out, as I knew it would be, licking the poisoned air for a final taste. "Don't make that ugly face," he used to tell me. "You never know when it'll freeze."

What I remember about my father's handsome face, when he was alive, is that his eyes could light up and twinkle—when he took us to Roger Williams Park, when we came home from camp, when he saw our report cards. Much of the rest of the time, his face wore a drawn look of effort, a look that made me feel guilty about the debt I knew I owed him, squeezed as he was between his problems at work and his debacle at home.

Some nights, after a scotch or two, if he didn't fall asleep on the couch in front of the TV, if he and Lola invited friends over to play cards, he put on a happy face, a boyish face, and told jokes. He poked fun, like Don Rickles, only not funny. Mostly, he made cracks that were meant to be endearing; but with me, there was always enough truth in his jibes to wound. Or maybe I just hadn't learned yet how to laugh at myself.

What I owe him and can never repay is the gorgeous education he worked his ass off to give me. The Connecticut border was where my two roads diverged, and Mort paid the tolls on the highway that led out of town. And that, as the poet said, has made all the difference.

Lola and I have another round of tea and kiss Harvey good-bye, and when we get to the parking lot, his secretary comes running after us to deliver a rough transcript of Lola's deposition, so she can approve it for accuracy, "unless she wants to waive that right."

I wrap both hands around the document and pull, devouring it as soon as we're in the car.

Q: I'm going to show you an operator's manual that was found on the boat. Have you ever seen it before, Mrs. Hornstein?
A: No.
Q: Look at page one, please. Do you see some handwriting on the page that says "T-Joint"?
A: Uh-huh.
Q: Is that handwriting familiar to you? Is it your husband's handwriting?
A: I don't know.
Q: Well, do the best you can. Do you recognize the handwriting?
A: No. I don't.

The opposition attorney asked repeatedly whether she recognized various samples of Mort's handwriting. Twenty questions, coming at her again and again from different angles. "No," she said. "No, I don't think so." The more he asked, the firmer she got, and three pages later, she was "absolutely certain" that the handwriting couldn't possibly be Mort's.

Q: Do you remember seeing your husband change any parts on the *Mr. Fix It*?
A: I can't remember.
Q: Did he do maintenance on the boat?
A: Maybe. I think so.
Q: What kind of maintenance did he do?
A: I don't know.
Q: All you can say is that he might have done some work on the vessel, but you don't know what, specifically?
A: Yes.
Q: Did he have a tool kit or anything that he kept on the boat?
A: He had some tools.
Q: Did you ever see him replace a part on the generator?
A: I don't remember.
Q: Do you recognize this handwriting?
A: Definitely not.

Now I know why Harvey didn't want me looking over Lola's shoulder in the conference room, and why he's probably hoping I'll be on the next plane to Paris. I'd have turned Mort in whether he was guilty or not.

Q: Do you remember what the weather was like on the day of the accident? Was it cold?
A: I think so.
Q: So he turned on the generator?
A: I don't know. I don't know what he did.
Q: Did you usually run the generator for heat when you were at the dock?
A: At the dock, we usually hooked up to the shore power.
Q: Do you know why your husband might have used the generator this time, instead of the shore power?

A: I don't know. He must have had his reasons.
Q: He took care of those things and you just relied on him?
A: Yes. I relied on him for everything.
Q: Do you have any actual memory of the day this incident happened?
A: I remember it was very cold and we made love—
Q: You don't need to tell us personal things.
A: Okay.
Q: What's the next thing you remember?
A: About four days later, I woke up in the hospital, and I had this thing in my arm, and I was missing my nail polish, and I didn't know why.
Q: Do you still see any doctors for the injuries you sustained in the accident?
A: I see Dr. Moore.
Q: What kind of doctor is he?
A: Just the regular kind. He's not a psychiatrist.
Q: Do you feel you have any continuing problems as a result of the incident?
A: I can't remember things.
Q: You feel your memory is impaired?
A: Yes.
Q: Is there anything else you feel?
A: I don't feel that I have any brain damage, although some people say I do. I think I'm lucky. But my memory is bad. Maybe that's from the brain damage.
Q: But other than loss of memory, there's nothing else that—
A: No.
Q: —that afflicts you?
A: I'm fine. I don't limp. I don't stutter.
Q: You speak well.
A: I'm very lucky. I'm fine.

Q: You have your coordination and everything else?
A: I get a little dizzy some times.
Q: Do you have any hobbies?
A: I knit. I play golf. But I'm not so good anymore.
Q: Anything else?
A: I play a lot of cards.
Q: Do you do any boating?
A: I stay away from boats. Boats aren't so good in my family.

In the remaining hours before I have to be at the airport to head back to Paris, I'd like to conduct a little interrogation of my own. But Lola refuses to discuss the deposition or anything else, because she wants to make an unscheduled trip back to the East Side to see the rabbi. "Seeing the rabbi" has never been a good sign.

"Start the car," she says. "Hurry up."

I suggest taking a minute to peek at the Caddy's exhaust system, just to see if Mort stuffed anything into the muffler.

"The car's fine. We're in a rush."

Lola's just decided she needs to change her Hebrew name. While she's telling me to "step on it," she relates "an ancient Jewish myth," one that's news to me—and for all I know, she could be making it up as she goes along—that changing your name can save your life. That the angel of death comes down from heaven with an engraved invitation with one particular name on it, and if he can't find a perfect match for that name, then he leaves empty-handed. Some day in the future, she says, that angel will come calling for Leibalah, but she'll answer only to Molke.

"It's a neat trick if it works," I say, thinking it's too bad no one told Mort. "But do you think the angel of death is a moron? You think he speaks only Hebrew?"

"So I should change Lola, too?" she asks.

"If he really wanted you, he'd have taken you from the boat. He was already there anyway, picking up Daddy. So what's the point of changing your name now?"

She doesn't answer. But who am I to argue? Hell, I changed my name, too.

So I head for the temple and ask if she wants to stop by the cemetery on the way—to say good-bye to Mort. We have time, and she's never been to his grave.

"No."

"You don't want to visit Daddy's grave?"

"No."

The summer sky is darkening and it's beginning to rain. I can feel the barometric pressure falling, and it makes me reach for questions I would normally have considered out of bounds, not because I'm reluctant to intrude but because I don't usually want to hear the answers.

"Why don't you want to visit Daddy's grave?"

She's silent for a minute and then she blurts it out.

"I blame him. I blame him for the accident."

A clap of thunder sounds; then the hail begins—spit-size balls that sound like they're denting the hood, followed by golf balls that could crack a windshield. I pull over into the breakdown lane behind a long line of faintly visible cars whose hazard lights are flashing. The hail goes *rat-a tat-tat* on the roof, like it's the end of the world.

Big tears are streaming down Lola's face. It's the first time I've seen her cry since the accident, and there's a look of astonishment where she normally wears the zombie mask.

"What's wrong?"

"Hail!"

"Don't worry, we're safe in the car."

"God's punishing me."

"That's silly. Why would God do that?"

"Because I just told the truth about Mort."

"How could the hail be connected to Daddy? What about everyone else who had to pull off the road?"

"What do you think *they* said about Mort?"

"Mom, this is just weather. We're not in the Old Testament. It's not a message from God, and it's not the 'truth about Mort.' "

But as soon as I repeat her words, it hits me, *me*, rigid, card-carrying rationalist me, that maybe she's right. Maybe there *is* a connection between the hail and the "truth about Mort."

Wasn't she right about the jelly beans?

It could be argued, and it was, that Mort was just a casualty of the salty ocean breeze, of the corroded connection between two rust-pitted pipes. The generator was, in fact, the material cause of his death; it was death's go-between, its conduit. The T-joint was its medium, the gas its instrument. We can thank Aristotle for deconstructing causality and forcing us to finer explanations, for not letting us off the hook with a merely mechanical account. He parsed the shopworn grammar of cause and effect, separating the role of the match from that of the spark and the woodpile, identifying the *what* and the *how* and the *why*, so he could ultimately point a finger at the *who*. He taught us to follow the chain of causality to its origin, until we find its agent.

After Lola told Mort she was cold, after he got out of their berth to turn on the heat, it was Mr. Fix It's feckless fingers that turned a simple emission system into a gas chamber. He made the venom flow out of the life-sucking rust hole. He battened down the loose-fitting hatches and left the generator running without a bilge blower, with the boat tucked into its slip. He spun the toxic cocoon.

At his funeral, his lifelong best friend—his cousin Sid—

who played bad Joey Bishop to Mort's bad Don Rickles—threw his arms around me and wept. Wept for the loss of a man who'd been as dear to him as a limb. Then Cousin Sid sat me down in a corner and told me a story, his shoulders heaving. Something I needed to hear, he said. The week before he died, my father had shown up at Sid's office, unexpectedly. Mort said there was something on his mind that he needed to discuss. They sat down across from each other at Sid's desk, but when Mort began to speak, he started to cry. And then he couldn't—or wouldn't—say what he'd come to say, and he sat there with Sid and just cried and cried for an hour.

I waited for Sid to dry his own eyes and tell me what was going on, as he must have waited for my father to do that day. But Mort never stopped crying, Sid said, and he left without putting his burdens into words. A week later, he was dead. And Sid couldn't help wondering.

"Do you think he might have planned it?" Sid asked me—first giving me the terrible news of my father's despondency, then adding to it a repugnant, unverifiable suspicion of his own.

I couldn't answer Sid about my father that day; I couldn't have found the words, any more than my father could. Suicide was, after all, my first thought when Ben called me, when I imagined Mort sticking his head in the boat's nonexistent oven. Helen admitted jumping to the same conclusion.

But once I saw the evidence, all the bread crumbs that were strewn along the way, I knew that his death was "an accident," a collision between negligence and happenstance. He surely had a hand in his own demise, but the hand was inadvertent. And I'll bet he took plenty to his grave that he couldn't say out loud to anybody, including Sid.

Is there a special afterlife for hapless handymen? Some spot where everything is eternally unfixable, where glue won't stick and staples won't hold? If so, Mort is there, deactivated, his only tools the toy screwdriver Ben pitched into his grave and the frayed Mr. Fix It badge from Helen. In my father's hereafter, spark plugs won't spark, engines wheeze but won't start, switches can't be switched or rewired, and no more damage can be done.

May he rest in peace.

FIFTEEN

Candyland

TEN YEARS LATER

My antiperspirant crusade was a failure in France, as tourists even today can attest. My efforts to "migrate" the French from old-world to new-world hygiene, from artisanal to processed cheese, from Dijon to ballpark mustard, from warm baguettes to shelf-stable dough—all of them failed. Undeterred, I blazed bold trails into one blind cul-de-sac after another, shepherding products the French evinced no need for. It turned out to be my specialty.

Not long after I lost my Gallic Wars, I was called back to the home office in New York, crowned senior vice president and put in charge of a whole portfolio of "niche" brands. These were products that might have been big, that promised to soar but sank, several of them under my own earlier stewardship. The whole dismal collection was what my generous new boss, a man who reminded me of Jimmy Stewart, called "Promising

Failures." Oh, he could spin. But every single one was a *loser*—and its only reason for being was that it still had billings. Which is what we all lived and died for.

Included in the portfolio was a product I'd launched before I moved to Paris, an effervescent toilet-bowl scrub, created with the same technology that was used for the client's best-selling denture cleanser. Repurposing the capital equipment, as it were. The creative director had insisted on advertising Bubble-Scum's excellent manufacturing pedigree—"Let's tell 'em Bubble-Scum is from the people who make Dental-Dolly"—a dual strategy that drowned Bubble-Scum's early promise and nearly flushed Dental-Dolly down the toilet, too.

Five years later, I was surprised to see that both brands were still on marketing life support, and my job was to keep the client from pulling the plug.

Hallelujah, back to meaningful work.

Today, my mind is a compendium of facts and minutiae about carbon monoxide. I can describe its molecular composition, its intended use in metallurgy, the speed with which it fuses with hemoglobin—an *un*intended use—and its side effects in victims. Blood was made for oxygen, but it's fiendishly attracted to carbon monoxide. Their molecules make an unholy alliance, like a pair of doomed lovers, suffocating blood from the inside out, like a pillow held tightly over the face, only from the inside. Because Lola slept by a leaky porthole that Mort had "repaired," she survived, and some parts of her are the better for it. A single night in the boat's poisoned crypt accomplished what years of shock treatment had not: Aunt Flossie never takes over her thinking anymore. Bill was finally smothered. The cherry never pops up. I'm not recommending poisonous gas as a therapeutic option in manic depression, but it had an unintended benefit in this case.

Where is the center of the universe now? Ask a cosmologist and you'll get the standard reply: There *is* no center of the universe—the big bang blew everything out equally, and there are no privileged positions. But let him step into Lola's force field and perhaps he'll give a different reply. The center of the universe is in a condo in Boca—in a gated pastel community on a manicured golf course where the villas are pink and turquoise and the golfers dress to match them. The sun always shines. Happy hour starts at 4:00 p.m., and there's a buffet three times a day.

Before her wrongful-death suit got to court, the deep pockets paid up. In fact, everyone who ever touched the frigate *Mr. Fix It* had to kick in something. Liability being relative, Mort was deemed partially responsible for his death, but, as Harvey said, "Juries never put *all* the blame on the victim."

It's hardly the route she would have chosen, but that's how Lola's ship came in.

Now she lives with two loyal companions: Ramona, a Maltese with indelible tearstains and an overbite, and, of course, the eponymous Pussy.

But she no longer lives with Eddie Silverman, "the big shot in air-conditioning" who took her to Florida. Their first year together, he went to the market, the car wash, the bank, and the dry cleaner's, while she played canasta and golf with her friends.

"Slow down," he urged her one day when she was driving her golf cart. "There's someone up ahead who doesn't look so good." The man in question was about eighty, gray-faced, and slumped over the wheel of his own golf cart in the middle of a fairway.

"He's just napping," Lola said.

The cart got a little closer, and Eddie got a better look. "I think he's dead."

"What can *we* do?" Lola said. "We'll miss our tee-off."

And away she drove.

Five holes later, they heard the sirens.

But Eddie didn't last long, either. In their second year together, he had a quadruple bypass ("all five sides," she told me, alarmed), but by then he'd accomplished his mission—he'd nagged her back into the flow.

Every year, she gets less cotton-headed, and while she's not exactly a live wire yet, at least she doesn't short-circuit anymore. The new Lola is a bit dotty, but maybe that's not such a terrible thing. And as Ben always says, time will tell. Maybe this, too, shall pass. With her chipper smile and fire-and-ice lips, if she weren't just a little bit *off*, she could turn into Kitty Carlisle Hart.

So the men have been like buses. After Eddie was buried, Jack "the Phantom" came along, earning his nickname because he didn't live a year. Both men left their color-coordinated furniture behind, so her formerly airy all-white condo now has a black leather den and a forest green living room.

After the Phantom passed, Lola started calling herself "the Black Widow." But nothing has stopped the suitors. Harry Schwartz, a handsome man of seventy-five, who's probably next, jokes he'll never kiss her on her lips—again. He has great comic timing, and she says he's the love of her life—she finally got a Jewish doctor—but apparently he isn't feeling so well, either.

"I had a terrible scare the other day," she told me over the phone. "Harry was supposed to pick me up for dinner, but he never showed up. I kept calling his condo, but there was no answer."

"So you went over to check on him?"

"I'd have missed dinner. As it was, I had to go out alone."

"How *could* you!"

"Don't worry, I never dropped out of the Singles Club."

She's always telling me not to worry, and in this case I don't, because she's *president* of the Singles Club. And from that lofty position, she continues to espouse her lifelong matrimonial Lola-isms—the commandments that her children are also expected to observe.

It's better to marry and divorce than never to marry at all. Helen took that advice to heart, marrying and divorcing her high school boyfriend and then his successor. And it's true, she does seem a lot happier now.

Ben married a beautiful blond shiksa I call "Violetta"—she's got a dazzling soprano and a nagging cough. Meanwhile, he's recorded the Grieg piano concerto and built a medical practice so full of musicians that his waiting room looks like backstage at Carnegie Hall.

I, however, resisted Lola's marital drumbeat—enduring one romantic failure after another—and concluded that the uncoupled life was still worth living. I wasn't much for settling, or for settling down, and besides, by the time I was in my forties, the men weren't exactly like buses.

Husbands don't give hickeys. This was not an argument against hickeys per se, but Lola's idea of a character test. Unfortunately, I never knew whether it was a way to tell if my boyfriend was actual husband material, or if it meant marriage would take the hickey out of any man. (The jury is still out.)

Never marry a good dancer. Growing up, this rule baffled me, since Mort had a display case of brass dancing trophies in our cellar. And both of Helen's ex-husbands danced, which I guess just proves the point. I still don't really get it.

But one day about a year ago, into my office walked an intriguing man who said he hadn't danced since his Bar Mitzvah—and then he'd danced only once, because his father made him dance with his mother. I didn't know why he was telling me this—the commercial he was supposed to direct had two dance scenes in it—and arguably he was disqualifying himself. But I liked his story, and I imagined teaching him to dance would be a lot of fun.

I followed him out to the preproduction meeting in Vancouver, an event that was usually covered by an assistant account executive about six levels my junior. At dinner the first night, I found myself at a table for eight, with Mr. Right on my left. My Caesar salad came without the sine qua non, anchovies—the waitress said there were none left in the kitchen. Meanwhile, Mr. Right excused himself, and when he came back to the table a few minutes later, he put a small paper bag in front of me. Inside were two cans of anchovies, one flat, one rolled, from a nearby gourmet store.

Then he handed me a can opener. "Once in a while," he said, "the key on the tin breaks."

That did it. I didn't need another sign.

Yet there was another sign. He's handy—he's *really* handy—meaning the things that he fixes stay fixed. And lately he's begun to intercede when I try to do my own small repairs, reminding me that I'm Mr. Fix It's daughter. Too bad he wasn't around the night of my friend Tessa's birthday party, when I threw a switch in her circuit-breaker box to try to get her dishwasher going again and instead brought down the electricity in her entire apartment building.

Alas, one potential deal breaker is Mr. Right's boat, a classic mahogany runabout from the sixties, with a Corvette engine and a "velvet drive" that he maintains himself. As Lola said in her deposition, "boats aren't so good in our family." And once she finds out about it, she'll drive him nuts until he gets rid of it.

"Does he have any idea what he's getting into?" one of my friends whispered to one of his friends, who repeated it to him.

He laughed and I pretended to.

He puts up with all of it, and I think he's a saint.

(Also, so far, no hickeys.)

When we were kids, during the early crazy years, my siblings and I hid under a blanket and put the soles of our feet together at night. We called ourselves the Toes Club. Vonnegut called it *boko-maru*—"joining the soles to connect the souls"—and I swear it worked. The Aphasia Hope Society was its natural evolution. Sibling syndrome was its manifestation. We're too old to put our feet together now, in our forties, but Ben and Helen and I are still aligned—especially when it comes to our mother.

Recently, she wanted to take out a $100,000 home equity loan with two points so she could enter a $500 jingle-writing contest at her bank. "What would you do with the money?" I asked her. "Put it in the bank," she said.

Her math skills still have a way to go, and she can't add people up, either. But since I'm in charge of her financial affairs, she sends me an accounting in the mail once a month, on a scrap of paper or the back of a ripped envelope.

> *So what do you think of this? Some woman named Angela called me and said I won a sweepstakes from playing in 1983, and the money was never sent to me. It's about 3½ million dollars. And it won't cost me anything but their commission. They will deposit the money in my bank account as soon as my check to them clears. I already put it in the mail.*

I canceled her checking account.

Regardless, she's back to running things. She's chief fund-raiser for the hospice where Eddie and Jack died, and she raises money by "streetwalking"—her word for running around Boca and Palm Beach to solicit donations for her benefits. At least I think that's what she means.

The rest of the time, she's on the golf course. She positions herself on the first tee and hits a few balls until one lands where she wants it, and that's the ball she plays. Everyone goes along with her rules. A ball in the sand trap gets an automatic do-over, and anything within a foot of the pin counts as "in." If she plays really badly, she asks for her money back. So far, there have been no complaints about her shaving points off her score or moving her ball from the rough to the fairway when she thinks no one's looking. "I only do that with family," she assures me.

When she moved to Boca, she taught her neighbors how to play canasta so she'd have a game, and then they taught her how to play bridge.

"I play a hand just fine," she tells me; "I just can't remember the cards."

"How's your bidding?" I ask.

"I like to open with three points."

What could explain the fact that she wins? I ask if she's gone back to taking cards from the discard pile.

"I don't need to. I'm getting better, while the rest of them are getting worse."

She could be right. The last time I saw the women in her card group, one of them asked me three times who I was. As she was leaving, she asked me who Lola was.

Like the old Lola and the mid-stage Lola, the new Lola is a big reader, and she started a Cultural Committee in her community.

"What are the topics?" I ask her.

"How good we are," she replies.

"Well, what are the goals?"

"Not to be swallowed up by the Entertainment Committee."

"That's nice," I say.

When she was named editor in chief of the writing club, I asked her to send me her stories. "We don't write them down," she said.

So I explained that writings are always written down, and since then, I get something in the mail every day. Given her preoccupation with food, she sends a lot of recipes—scribbled on the backs of grocery receipts.

For her annual Yom Kippur party, Lola starts cooking before Purim, keeping her Crock-Pot going round the clock, then freezing everything, including the Minute rice, for six months. *Mmm mmm.* During this cooking marathon, I get urgent culinary calls. "What's that thing with salmon?" "How do I get this can open?" "Where's the broiler on my Crock-Pot?" But eventually it all comes back as poetry.

Even though I'm playing golf,
My Crock-Pot is at work.
While it cooks,
I'm on the green—
I told you I'm no jerk.
Burn the brisket on both sides
Tastes so good I'm full of pride.
Wine and ketchup make great sauce
On Yom Kippur, I'm the boss.

Unfortunately, Eddie and Jack didn't last long on her menu. Lola, queen of the Crock-Pot and angel of mercy, loved them to death—schmeering honey on their challah and burning their brisket on both sides—just the way they liked it.

Everything's fine here, so don't worry,
but Eddie needs a balloon in his heart.

Everything's fine here, so don't worry,
but Jack got cancer.

Everything's fine here, so don't worry,
but Harry has a lump in his stomach.

The men have been like buses, and they're still coming, but Lola is the last bus stop on the long highway to hospice.

Although the angel of death has been coming around for all the men in her life, so far Lola herself is deathproof. She speeds past the gatehouse of her country club, tailing the car in front of her while the barricade is in midair, and it regularly comes down on her roof. ("Everything's fine here, so don't worry, but maybe my car's not so good.") Early on, I had to trade in her convertible.

She drives her golf cart with the recklessness of an adolescent, pedal to the metal, swerving across steeply banked fairways with the depth perception of a Cyclops. I beg her to slow down when I visit—when I'm in the death seat.

"Don't worry, I'm just havin' a little fun."

A few weeks ago, she took a curve too fast and sent her picnic cooler hurtling into a canal. It flew through the air and landed with a thud in the water, she told me over the phone, and as it sank, she saw bubbles float to the surface. And then, under the bubbles, she saw the snout of an alligator.

"Mario! Mario!" she called to the groundskeeper.

And Mario dropped his hedge trimmer and came running to help the kind but uncoordinated Mrs. Hornstein.

"My cooler! My cooler's sinking! Take this," she said, pushing her ball retriever into his hand. "And hurry!"

"Oh, I don't think this will work, ma'am. The scooper's too small."

"So you'll have to go in, Mario?"

"Oh, I hope not, ma'am. I wouldn't want to do that. I'm scared of alligators."

"I'm sure there aren't any," she told him. "Now hurry!"

"How could you do that, Mom?" I asked her as she proudly recounted the episode. "How could you send that sweet old man into the canal when you'd just seen an alligator?"

"Well, maybe it wasn't an alligator."

"So you were lying to me just now? Or were you lying to Mario at the time?"

"Maybe my eyes were playing tricks on me."

When a liar tells you she *might* be lying, is she telling the truth? I wasn't sure what to believe.

"You knew you were sending that man into an alligator-infested swamp! You were practically bragging about it a minute ago!"

"Don't exaggerate. It worked out just fine, didn't it? I got my cooler back and I tipped him big. Anyway, alligators never hurt people."

Who's to say why some traits return and others do not, why her instinct to lie is coming back with force but a sense of morality is not? I like to think that the lying part of her brain was so well developed, it was too hard to kill. Maybe that's the essence of character.

But there are accidents. Lola fell off a curb in Palm Beach a few days ago, "streetwalking," toppling out of her three-inch heels while carrying a Mixmaster, and she broke a rib. After taking pain medication, she got dizzy and fell a second time at home. This afternoon, the doctor gave her a walker.

Her phone call catches me in LA on the set of "a commercial extravaganza" for Dental-Dolly—the agency's last, desperate effort to force-feed the brand. We're filming the reunion of two washed up celebrities who famously hated each other in their prime, and while their on-screen chemistry was always rotten, it's only gotten worse pitching dentures. He, a renowned sitcom father whose TV show was canceled thirty years ago, arrived on our set packing a gun, and he's been in the parking lot all morning taking target practice on Coke bottles. She, at breakfast, stirred vodka into her coffee with her dentures. A faded beauty queen with a legendary bustline, she nearly drank herself to death last year between takes of an eighteen-hour-bra commercial that went on for over a week.

This shoot has the potential to be the highlight, and the twilight, of my career.

Meanwhile, when I ask Lola if she needs anything, she says, "Come right away. Come tomorrow."

"Are you in pain? Are you still dizzy? Are you out of food or something?"

"I've got enough food for breakfast."

I book a seat on the red-eye and turn into Lassie.

On my way from the airport to her condo, I'm supposed to "pick up a few things" at Famous Deli, where dozens of waistless seniors are fighting over specials. Dressed entirely in black in a pastel world, I pretend I'm here with Woody Allen, casting. My shopping list, dictated by Lola, includes all the major Jewish food groups.

> Two pounds of potato salad, two pounds of corned beef—the extra-fatty kind, don't get lean, it has no taste—six stuffed cabbages, a dozen knishes, a pound

of chopped liver, and a couple of chubs. Better make it six chubs.

I pull up to her condo midafternoon with a small suitcase and three huge food bags. She must be redecorating before Harry moves in, because both his predecessors' tchotchkes now fill the garage. Lining one wall is Eddie's fat Buddha shrine and his collection of hard-to-find air-conditioner parts. Jack's discarded Barcalounger is still open, and I can almost hear him snoring in it. Next to these artifacts of love lost—and on top of a trash bin—I spot Lola's shiny new aluminum walker. Apparently, she's had a speedy recovery. Or I've been snookered.

Lola herself is in the kitchen—in pink curlers, white underwear, and black wedgies, with a pedometer around her ankle—balancing herself on a shaky stool to reach crystal goblets at the top of a cabinet, which she's pulling on to hoist herself up. I can feel the cabinet crashing down on both of us.

"Get down, Mom. You have to get down right now! Look at what you're wearing!"

And she descends immediately, always so cooperative, and takes off her bra.

"I meant your wedgies."

When she runs off to get flats, I unload the bags, expecting to find "enough food for breakfast." The refrigerator is crammed with doggie bags and Chinese takeout. The freezer's loaded with casseroles and pot roasts, and the walk-in pantry is prepped for hurricanes.

Apparently, the new Lola has given me a dose of the old *tootsanoo mootsanoo* and I fell for it. That was her code word for wheedling and sweet talk, her own brand of manic manipulation, so whatever Lola wanted, Lola got. It was the gentle force at the center of the universe, and in her prime, she could persuade the wind to change direction.

I didn't know she still had it in her, but it seems that the old *tootsanoo mootsanoo*, like Lola herself, is making an unexpected comeback.

What could be next?

"We've gotta leave right now," she tells me, "or we'll miss the early bird at the club."

After dinner, she jokes with the waiter, her favorite, that she'd like to take him home with her. Instead, we go to Burdines, which is open late for the annual bathing suit sale. The cruise department is crowded with bargain hunters of both sexes, seniors who are slouch-shouldered from leaning over golf balls and all-you-can-eat buffets. Lola disappears into a dressing room, and while I'm standing at the cash register in the middle of the floor, talking to a sales clerk, a boy of about twenty, she walks up in her white nylon underpants, her thighs jiggling like Flub-a-Dub, and asks him to get her a bigger size. I'm apoplectic.

"What do you care?" she says. "We don't even know him."

Later that night, when I'm in her guest room—which has been decorated for ten years, mysteriously, with expensive frames that still have the store photos in them—I overhear her on the phone, reeling off numbers like a bookie. First her Social Security number, then the one on her American Express card.

"Who was that?"

"Walter."

"Who's Walter?"

"I don't know him."

"What did he want?"

"He has a five-thousand-dollar package for me, so he needs my credit card."

"Is it something you ordered?"

"No, he's giving it to me."

"Mom, that's a scam. Walter is a crook."

"He is *not*. He's Jewish."

"So were your aunts and uncles."

"He just needs my credit card for identification."

"But he called *you*. Shouldn't he be giving you identification?"

"Don't worry, I do this all the time. It'll be fine."

I cancel her credit cards.

The next day, my siblings show up. Apparently, we all got the old *tootsanoo mootsanoo*, and everyone saluted, reporting for duty, bearing food. Helen got the distress call from her dizzy, starving mother last night, when I was already here and had stored two new doggie bags from dinner in the fridge. She canceled her patients and her classes, jumped on a plane, and went straight to *Famous*, with her two children in tow. The five-year-old is carrying a knapsack full of seeds and nuts as self-defense—she became a vegetarian after spending Christmas vacation alone with Lola, who "spoiled" her with hot dogs three times a day for a week.

Ben arrives later with Violetta and their six-year-old, Donny, who is unlikely to escape his musical roots. She went into labor with him in the audience at the Metropolitan Opera House during Lucia's "Mad Scene." Dame Joan Sutherland was nailing the high E-flat in a historic performance, but afterward, in her dressing room, she asked why the madness in Row D was competing with that on stage. It was a snowy night, impossible to get a taxi, and as the curtain came down, the performance manager was still pacing back and forth with Violetta in the foyer, waiting for an ambulance, joking about the musical future of a child born at the Met. Predictably, Donny is developing an angelic voice, and even without a crystal ball, I can see a von Trapp family act in their future.

The evening they all arrive, to celebrate, we put aside the redundant deli fare and get takeout from the best Chinese restaurant in Boca. Lola lights Shabbos candles and puts the flaming pou-pou platter on her silver lazy Susan. Before we get to the table, she's devoured the spareribs, while Ben tries to talk her out of drinking.

"You know, Mom, liquor is a central nervous system depressant."

"I'm not drinking," she says, pouring herself some Pinot Grigio.

"That's your second glass."

"I don't consider wine to be liquor."

"But wine *is* liquor."

"Not to *me*."

Between moo shu pork and shrimp with lobster sauce, Donny puts aside his sheet music to practice for his spelling bee.

"I always won that," Lola tells him.

Donny has an audiographic memory and can parrot back the dialogue from dozens of movies, TV shows, and commercials. Could it be a touch of Lola's brain? I hope not, but I plan to test him myself.

"Donny, the first word is *conceited*," I say.

But before he has a chance to answer, Lola interrupts. "It means stuck-up."

"Not you, Mom; this is Donny's test. Can you use the word in a sentence, Donny?"

Lola says, "*She's* stuck-up."

"No, the word is *conceited*, and it's Donny's turn, not yours, okay?"

Donny spells. "C-O-N-C-I-E-T-E-D."

"Good!" Lola says.

"No, it isn't; that's not right," I say.

"It's good enough!"

"Mom, please, I'm the judge."

"You're *always* the judge," she says.

I roll my eyes, and as I turn my head, I glance in the mirror behind me and catch her doing the same thing. The dramatic tension between us has been reduced to mimicry.

Ben takes over. "The next word is *bizarre*."

"*Bizarre?*" Donny says, "That means strange."

"And it's a place to buy things," Lola adds.

"No, that's *bazaar*."

"Well, it's close enough," she insists. "Don't be such nit-pickers."

And so it goes. Half-right is fine. Wrong is good, too. Nothing is absolute anymore, because her standards keep stretching as her capacity contracts. Since the accident, tolerance is up and expectations are down. And that seems like a very good thing.

The sunset is reflecting in the sliding glass door beside the dining table, and while we're drinking tea, something thumps against the glass and drops to the ground. There, lying on the grass, is a dying bird, beak down, its beautiful black-and-white-speckled wings splayed open like an angel of death's. The beak opens, the bird takes a final breath, and then it stops moving altogether.

Pussy walks up to the glass and meows.

All eyes turn to Dr. Ben, man of the house, carver of turkeys, filleter of fish—and reformed bunny killer. He puts on a pair of work gloves and *prepares himself* to deal with the dead bird before Pussy can get to it. And as he reaches down to grab it by its tail, the bird squawks, and Ben jumps back and the rest of us gasp. Then it rights itself and hobbles a few feet on the grass before flying away. Phoenix rising.

"And another thing," Lola says to Ben. "If I ever have

another accident, don't pull the plug so fast just 'cause my brain is dead. My brain always comes back."

"Don't worry," he says, "we'll give your brain to science."

"I better be dead longer than that bird."

After dinner, Ben performs a hilarious deadpan rendition of "Feelings," with Lola accompanying him at the keyboard. And then, after I soften her up with a bit of my own *tootsanoo mootsanoo*, I ask her if I can write her story.

"Write it *down*, you mean?"

"Yes. Like a biography."

After thinking about it over red bean ice cream and pineapple chunks, hers and mine, she says yes. "You'll never have better material."

She wouldn't be Lola if she didn't have suggestions—a list of lies she'd like to make sure I tell. "Don't forget Sol Hurok, okay?"

But by the time we finish the dishes, she gives in and says I can write the truth.

Or some of it.

"Do you have to tell the part about Bill?"

I'm stunned she brings Bill up. She's never said his name out loud to me before, and my knowledge of what Bill made her do came from eavesdropping during the worst of times. I thought he'd been snuffed out by the gas on the boat, but apparently he's making a bit of a comeback. And right after the *tootsanoo mootsanoo*.

Just when I thought it was safe to go back in the water.

"Don't you think we need the Bill part to make sense of the rest of it?" I ask.

She looks at me blankly.

The next morning, Lola wants to read what I've written so far, but I have to confess I haven't started.

A week later, a month later, six months later, she calls and asks me again.

"Mom, I need a little time, okay?"

"How much time? The Haggadah was written faster. Don't you at least have a title?"

"Not yet."

"How about *Love Story*?"

"Been done."

"Too bad. Ali MacGraw would be great as me."

"She's *eight* feet tall."

"How about Bette Midler?"

Once upon a time, Lola had a sparkle in her eye with more facets than a diamond, and a brain with more complications than a grandfather clock—even *her* grandfather's clock. She was a twisted Rubik's cube, unmalleable, solutionless, but she could calculate the odds of pairing up or straightening out faster than I could say "Ante up."

She was a boundless force of grandiose plans, an epidemic of reckless energy, and she used plenty of it to develop my talents. She was both grain of sand and pearl. I marched to the beat of her bipolar drummer—presto agitato or molto depressimo—and if occasionally there was a pause, an interval of tranquillity, it was only intermission. The old Lola was a force of nature who came up behind me as suddenly as a twister and turned Providence into Oz. She was the wind shear beneath my wings.

The new Lola is still spinning, but slowly, and the center of the universe is gone. Gone is the wind-whipped siren, the human sine curve, the widening gyre. Now that she's been neurologically derotated, she's as steady as the beat of a metronome.

So far anyway.

What I see in her face is more than happiness—it's acceptance. It didn't come from reflection or revelation. It stole in quietly and filled the vacant space that once held longing and regret. It's the thing with plucked feathers that's adjusted to hobbling.

I can't figure out how she does it—being so sanguine, so cheerful, despite her history and handicaps and the half-lives of her husbands, when the rest of the world feels entitled to limitless prospects.

"I keep my head down," she says. "I keep my eye on the ball. And I just keep swinging."

Acknowledgments

How lucky can you get? Lisa Bankoff, summa cum agent, shepherded my manuscript out of the literary wilderness and into the promised land. Louise Bernikow, mentor and magician, waved her literary wand over it, sparing future readers much unripe prose. Jordan Pavlin read the story while running a high fever and decided, before her fever broke, to publish it. I struck while the iron was hot. She is a dazzling editor with a dedicated team. Huge thanks to Carol Carson, Leslie Levine, Victoria Pearson, and Sarah Gelman at Knopf, and to Elizabeth Perrella at ICM.

Orin Wechsberg encouraged me to sit down and write this story, and then he demonstrated the patience of a saint when I didn't get up from the chair. (Reader, I married him.) "Helen, Ben, and Violetta Hornstein" shared their memories to burnish my own—they aided, abetted, and occasionally parodied my drafts, once, unforgettably, to music—and I will always be grateful they all have a sense of humor. For inspiring me with stories about the origin of our species, I am indebted to my cousin Lewis Pollock, who turned me into Nancy Drew. For close readings and friendship, good fortune sent me Bob Berenson, Terry Berenson, Vicki Coe, Arlyn Gardner, Sybil Mellion, Paul Solovay, Susan Spiegel Solovay, and Hunter Yager. Jane Fankhanel, "my attorney," was, as always, a counselor without peer.

MY MOTHER, MY MUSE—
the indomitable "Lola"—
told me I'd "never have better material."
She is the sine qua non.

Happy Mother's Day

I hope you like the card. I made it myself.

A NOTE ABOUT THE AUTHOR

Nancy Bachrach worked in advertising in New York and Paris, spinning hot air like cotton candy, glorifying her clients' beloved denture adhesives and powdered orange-juice substitutes. Before that, she was, sequentially, a clumsy waitress at Howard Johnson's, an overzealous customer-service rep fired for making genuine apologies, a stenographer for an insomniac poet, and a teaching assistant in the philosophy department at Brandeis University, where she was one chapter ahead of her class. She lives in New York City, and this is her first book.

www.nancybachrach.com

A NOTE ON THE TYPE

This book has been set in Goudy Old Style, perhaps the best known of the more than one hundred typefaces designed by Frederic William Goudy (1865–1947).

Composed by Creative Graphics, Inc.
Allentown, Pennsylvania

Printed and bound by R.R. Donnelley & Sons,
Harrisonburg, Virginia